Love, Luck and Lessons for Life

Traditional wisdom on life's big questions

RUTH BINNEY

David and Charles

Contents

Introduction

It is our fate to live in an uncertain world. And although, in this age of technology, there is much we can control, chance still plays a major hand in all our lives, as it has done for countless generations. Ever since I learnt, as a child, the magpie-rhyme 'one for sorrow, two for joy' I have been fascinated by superstitions, proverbs and sayings, their origins and associations and the many ways in which they affect us, whether we believe them or not.

This book, devoted to the many aspects of love and life, is an unashamedly eclectic mixture of superstitions, sayings and science, proverbs and psychology, fantasy, fact and history. It is concentrated on the things that are important to us all, from romance and courtship to our homes, health, happiness money and friendships. In looking back to the many myths and ancient beliefs that still colour the way we think today I have tried where possible, to reconcile modern knowledge with the old fashioned and 'folk' wisdom as passed down by our grandparents.

The results are often as amusing as they are informative, especially as they reveal the abiding concerns of past societies in relation to the things that absorb our attention today. What's more, many common themes emerge, from the desires for love to touch us, for luck to keep us healthy and safe from danger, to our wish to be able to foresee what the future holds. It also becomes clear that we still like to be in tune with the seasons, that old habits die hard, and that much of our fate lies in our own hands. And, whether we are religious or not, it is obvious that the values of good and evil, as well as the desire to enhance the one and ward off the other, are as significant today as they ever were.

My research for this book has led me down many avenues in town and country both real and imagined, but I have drawn especially on an abundance of 19th-century sources, including popular magazines of the time such as *Home Chat*, *The Girl's Own Paper* and *The Quiver*. Key books have included the invaluable Victorian manual *Enquire Within* and, from America, *The House and Home Practical Book,* Florence Howe Hall's *Social Customs* and Emily Post's *Blue Book*. I have trawled widely in second-hand bookshops and the shelves of the London Library for the snippets, sayings and quotes that help bring each subject to life, and received many helpful suggestions from both friends and family. I am particularly grateful to Diana Brooke and Ann Usborne for their encouragement and contributions.

My thanks also go to my husband Donald for his patience and encouragement and to my daughter Laura, not least for the additional insights she has provided into the ups and downs of love and life. Appreciation also to Neil Baber, Lewis Birchon and the team at David & Charles for their belief in the project and their help in making it happen, and to Beverley Jollands for her meticulous editing.

When I was a teenager in the 1950s the very height of romance was to listen – with a boyfriend of course – to Buddy Holly singing *Words of Love* cooped up in the intimate confinement of a record-store booth. Little did I know then how lucky, in many respects, my life would turn out to be. As for life's lessons, those are still very definitely 'work in progress'!

Ruth Binney

Love

A life without love, both given and taken, is empty indeed.

So vital is love to our lives, and so powerful are its effects, that it can raise us to the dizziest heights of emotions while without it we can literally waste away in body and in spirit. No wonder, then, that since ancient times people have seen love as a gift from the gods and made it the stuff of fairytales. Or that love has inspired everything from the world's greatest art and literature to the most saccharine love poems and songs.

That falling in love is also the necessary prelude to the continuance of the human race is, of course, the biological drive behind our emotions. And, as Buddy Holly so famously sang 'It's so easy to fall in love'. This does not make falling in and out of love any less painful, nor necessarily ensure that the partner we choose is our perfect match. Long gone, though, are the days when, while an unmarried man was a 'bachelor gay', spinsterhood was a state that was deeply pitied, if not despised. No wonder, then, that dozens of customs, rituals and superstitions are associated with the finding and keeping of a partner, from the 'marriage market' that was the London Season to the sending of anonymous Valentine cards to ways of conjuring up the face of your lover in a dream.

Such is the fickleness of human nature that, in Shakespeare's eloquent phrasing 'the course of true love never did run smooth.' Hearts and promises are broken, aspirations shattered. Yet more reasons, from the first kiss, for wanting staying in love, through courtship and into marriage, and for the underlying significance of every word and token that lovers exchange.

The Nature of Love

The bliss and pain of love go far beyond the mundane facts of physiology to evoke the deep emotions that inspire everything from pop singles to great literature. Long term, love is the cement that binds men and women, parents, children and families together.

HEART OVER HEAD

To fall in love is to let passion rule, and both our emotions and our hormones can get out of control. While love at first sight may well lead to a lifetime of married bliss, a more rational assessment of a couple's compatibility is the safer (though by no means infallible) option.

The difficulty of handling the emotions that sexual attraction generates was satirically summed up by the 16th-century humanist Erasmus of Rotterdam: 'Jupiter has bestowed far more passion than reason [and] ... set up two raging tyrants in opposition to Reason's solitary power: anger and lust ... Reason does the only thing she can and shouts herself hoarse, repeating formulas of virtue, while the other two bid her go hang herself, and are increasingly noisy and offensive, until at last their Ruler is exhausted, gives up and surrenders.'

For some lucky people, passion continues throughout married life. In her famous book *Married Love*,

John Gray, author of the bestselling Men Are From Mars, Women Are From Venus, *believes that the way to keep passion alive is to artificially boost the levels of specific body chemicals – for men dopamine, the hormone that surges though the body in the early, passionate stages of a relationship, for women serotonin, the chemical that controls their feelings and increases both confidence and energy.*

first published in 1918, Marie Stopes anticipates such bliss with the sentiment that from desires of the flesh spring '… not only the wonder of a new bodily life [a child], but also the enlargement of the horizon of human sympathy and the glow of spiritual understanding which a solitary soul could never have attained alone.'

LOVE'S MEANING

There is more to love than a mere catalogue of physiological responses, essential though these are to procreation. The Greeks had two words for it, and it has been the subject of countless works of literature.

Love, when obsessive and all-consuming, conforms to the Greek *eros*. This, argues Robin Norwood in her 1985 book *Women Who Love Too Much*, is love that engenders feelings of anxiety and tension, mystery and yearning, because the

WORDS OF LOVE

Some classic lines on what love means and how it is expressed:

* 'If thou must love me, let it be for nought
  Except for love's sake only …' (Elizabeth Barrett Browning)
* 'Love was to feel you in my very heart and hold you there for ever, through all chance and earthly changes.' (Robert Browning)
* '… love is not love/Which alters when it alteration finds.' (William Shakespeare)
* 'Love is life's end, an end, but never ending,
  All joys, all sweets, all happiness awarding …' (Edmund Spenser)
* 'To love is to pardon everything.' (Old French proverb)

beloved is prepared to undergo pain and suffering in the cause of love. *Agape*, by contrast, is the love of a committed partnership, in which two people share the same goals, values and interests. This is love in which friendship, companionship, comfort, devotion and understanding are key.

BY SCANNING WHAT GOES ON IN LOVERS' BRAINS, SCIENTISTS HAVE DISCOVERED THAT PEOPLE REALLY DO LOSE THEIR CRITICAL FACULTIES WHEN THEY FALL IN LOVE, MAKING THEM LESS ABLE TO SPOT FLAWS OR POTENTIAL PROBLEMS. THE PARTS OF THE BRAIN NORMALLY USED FOR MAKING ASSESSMENTS AND CRITICAL ANALYSIS BECOME DE-ACTIVATED, IT SEEMS, UNDER THE INFLUENCE OF THE EMOTIONAL SURGE THAT LOVE EVOKES.

LOVE AT FIRST SIGHT

It does happen, though we still don't know why: two people meet and instantly fall in love. But it may not be mutual. Very often it is the man who has to win his woman around.

It seems that the philosopher Bertrand Russell got it right when he wrote in *The Conquest of Happiness* (1930): 'On the whole women tend to love men for their character while men tend to love women for their appearance.' Psychological research bears out the fact that while for a man the body, hair, eyes and other visual attributes are the first factors in attraction, for a woman to be attracted to a man he must make her laugh, fit with her personality and treat her as she desires.

The painter Suzi Malin has made a serious study of the visual stimuli that draw men and women together at first sight and come up with three essential categories of attraction. In 'harmonism' the two people share similar proportions in their facial features. In 'echosim' (and to an extent in harmonism) faces echo each other in the shape of their upper eyelid line, their upper lip line and the shape or sweep of the eyebrow. In 'prima copulism' the attraction is to someone who resembles a person with whom they bonded early in life, most often a parent, but also, possibly, another close relative or a nanny.

When rationality takes over, love at first sight may turn out to be just infatuation. For it to grow into a permanent bond, friendship, mutual interests and compatible views on religion and other subjects are almost always essential.

LOVE'S UNWRITTEN LANGUAGE

Meeting the gaze of the love of your life across a room may be enough to signal your feelings, but there are long traditions involving rings, fans and gestures for exchanging a whole range of messages with would-be lovers.

According to the rules of the Victorian era, a gentleman who wants a wife should wear a ring

THE LANGUAGE OF FANS

How to send some messages of love:

'WHEN MAY I BE ALLOWED TO SEE YOU?' .... A closed fan touching the right eye.

'YOU MAY KISS ME.' .... A half-opened fan pressed to the lips.

'I LOVE ANOTHER.' .... Twirling the fan in the right hand.

'FORGIVE ME.' .... Hands clasped together holding an
open fan.

'I PROMISE TO MARRY YOU.' .... Shutting a fully opened fan slowly.

'DO NOT BETRAY OUR SECRET.' .... Covering the left ear with an open fan.

'WE ARE BEING WATCHED.' .... Twirling the fan in the left hand.

'DO YOU LOVE ME?' .... Presenting the fan shut.

on the first finger of his left hand, but should put it on the fourth finger if he intends never to marry. 'When,' says *Enquire Within*, 'a gentleman presents a fan, flower, or trinket to a lady with the left hand, this, on his part, is an overture of regard; should she receive it with the left hand it is considered as an acceptance of his esteem; but if with the right hand it is a refusal of the offer.' So, the guide explains, 'the passion of love is expressed' without the embarrassment of verbal exchanges.

The folding fan, invented by the Japanese and said to have been introduced to Europe by Catherine de Medici in the 16th century, is also used for communicating everything from 'You have won my love' when placed near the heart to 'I love you' when the eyes are hidden behind an open fan. The fan itself could also be decorated with fond messages such as 'Thoughts of you'.

MUSIC LOVERS

**Dubbed 'the food of love' by Shakespeare
in the opening lines of *Twelfth Night*, music
was inextricably linked with romance by the
troubadour poet-musicians of medieval Europe.**

The Bard makes many other references to the
power of music to heighten love, most notably
in *The Merchant of Venice* when, in response to
Jessica's complaint, 'I am never merry when I hear
sweet music,' her suitor Lorenzo reminds her of
the story of Orpheus, charming animals with his
music, and continues:

The man that hath no music in himself,
Nor is not mov'd with concord of
   sweet sound,
Is fit for treasons, stratagems and spoils;
The motions of his spirit are dull as night,
And his affections dark as Erebus.
Let no such man be trusted. Mark
   the music.

In France, from the 11th to the
14th centuries, troops of wandering
minstrels roamed the land, playing
and singing their songs of love and
chivalry. A 'fair lady who lay abed'
would be woken in the morning with
an aubade, and in the evening she would
be wooed again with a serenade.

> *To send his love in
> secret to an 'English
> rose' Mozart created
> coded messages in which
> musical notes were
> substituted for letters
> of the alphabet.*

THE FLUTE, NOT LEAST BECAUSE OF ITS SENSUAL SHAPE,
WAS AMONG THE EARLIEST MUSICAL INSTRUMENTS
ASSOCIATED WITH LOVE AND COURTSHIP. PLAYING
THEIR PIPES THE MUSICIANS OF ANCIENT MESOPOTAMIA
CREATED SOME OF THE WORLD'S FIRST HARMONIES.

CRYING OVER YOU

When love lets us down, it is only natural to shed tears of sadness, remorse and regret. 'Twas ever thus, but it seems that crying buckets really does do you good in the long run.

Charles Darwin believed that strong emotions make us cry because they make the small muscles around the eyes contract; today's experts believe that the crying reaction is a throwback to babyhood, when crying was our only means of communication. One of the latest theories, which comes from Dr William Frey of Minnesota, is that tears of sorrow (or joy) help to rid the body of irritant chemicals that build up during stress. And there's no doubt that a good cry really does make you feel better.

TEARS, CONTINUOUSLY PRODUCED IN SMALL QUANTITIES, ARE THE EYES' NATURAL LUBRICANTS. THE SALT THEY CONTAIN HELPS TO KILL BACTERIA AND OTHER AGENTS OF INFECTION THAT CAN INVADE AND DAMAGE THE EYES.

When love leaves, it's best not to cry for too long, as Shakespeare advises in *Much Ado About Nothing*:

Sigh no more, ladies, sigh no more
Men were deceivers ever,
One foot in sea and one on shore,
To one thing constant never.
Then sigh not so, but let them go,
And be you blithe and bonny;
Converting all your sounds of woe
Into Hey nonny nonny.

WHAT LOVERS WANT

Evolution has equipped us with the need to procreate and, in biological terms, this is why we fall in love. Of course it is all much more complicated than this, but there is no denying the needs of men and women for each other.

Countless surveys have attempted to discover what men and women most desire in a relationship. And while we have discovered that women like men who make them laugh, and men are attracted to women who boost their egos, much of it comes down to the 'basics' expressed in verse by William Blake in 1787:

The relationships researcher John Gottman believes it is possible to predict the chances of a couple's survival after eaves-dropping on just 15 minutes of their conversation. Key negatives he listens for are defensiveness, stonewalling, criticism and – most important of all – contempt.

What is it men in women do require?
The lineaments of Gratified Desire.
What is it women do in men require?
The lineaments of Gratified Desire.

Evolutionary psychologists say that, as in the natural world, conquest – particularly of a man

---

LOVING COUPLETS

A couplet-writing competition on love produced the following among more than 5,600 entries to the magazine Home Chat *in 1896:*

- If you'd have me and I'd have you,
  Why you'd be won and I'd be too.
- Loving is a painful thrill,
  And not to love more painful still.

- Remember, heart for heart was made
  And love alone with love is paid.
- Let money play a minor part.
  Have love alone to rule your heart.

over a potential rival – is an important element in the 'mating game'. A man who successfully steals a woman from a friend or enemy will also be playing to his animal instincts. Women, by the same token, love to be loved, flattered and treated well. In their eyes the alpha males are those who treat them best, both emotionally and materially.

BROTHERLY –
AND SISTERLY – LOVE

Within the family, sibling bonds may be tight or loose, and engender every emotion from solidarity to hate. Closest of all may be the bond between identical twins, who sometimes stay together for life.

The issue of loving one's brothers and sisters was neatly summed up in *Home Chat* magazine for 21 March 1896, which remarked that while sisters and brothers are 'not antagonistic in feeling' and would have 'chosen each other out as friends had they not had the close tie of relationship … much more frequently they are of varying nature … as the years roll on.'

Eulogizing sibling love, the piece, entitled 'Diversity of Characters', concluded rather sombrely: 'It is a beautiful sight to see a brother and sister, or two old women, bound by a double tie of blood and affection;

The ultimate in sibling rivalry: in murdering his brother Abel, Cain, son of Adam and Eve, showed how sibling love can turn to hate. After the killing, when he was asked by God where Abel was, Cain denied responsibility in his much-quoted reply: 'Am I my brother's keeper?'

who, having walked through life hand-in-hand,
can contemplate together with equanimity the
winter of their life on earth.'

Body and Mind

**Though fashions in body shape come and go, making oneself attractive
to the opposite sex is still, for most, an essential ingredient of falling
in love. The senses, especially sight, touch and smell, are particularly
powerful in triggering feelings of passion.**

THE BODY BEAUTIFUL

**As with the face, fashions in bodily beauty alter
with the era – the rounded, voluptuous bodies
favoured from the 16th to the 18th centuries,
and depicted in such paintings as Rubens'** *The
Three Graces,* **would be considered obese today.
However, the link between love and physical
beauty remains as strong as ever.**

The ideal of natural beauty was a Victorian
concept, inspired as a reaction against the elaborate
conventions of the 18th century. The 'health

BABIES, SCIENTISTS HAVE DISCOVERED, SPEND MORE
TIME LOOKING AT BEAUTIFUL THAN AT UGLY FACES.
A POSITIVE RESPONSE TO BEAUTY MAY HAVE EVOLVED,
IT IS THOUGHT, AS A WAY OF CHOOSING THE MOST
GENETICALLY ADVANTAGEOUS PARTNER.

---

and beauty' movement that began in the 1880s was at its peak in the 1930s, when women were advised that: 'Want of daylight, fresh air, and exercise, improper diet and laziness are beauty's enemies.' In the same era, Eddie Cantor, the Goldwyn Girls and Billy Barty sang, in the 1933 movie musical *Roman Scandals* that it was not just advisable, but your duty, to 'keep young and beautiful' if you wanted to be loved.

The concept of the beauty queen led to contests in seaside towns in Britain and country towns all over the USA. The first national competition, the Miss America Pageant of 1921, was a promotional gimmick devised by an Atlantic City hotel owner. It was won by Margaret Gorman, who bore a striking resemblance to the actress Mary Pickford. In Britain, the first Miss World competition was televised in 1959, 11 years after the first Miss Europe contest.

MY FACE IS MY FORTUNE

The face is always the focus of attention when two people meet and fall in love. Proverbially, the face is the index of the heart, and now scientists have discovered that there really does seem to be a universal standard of facial beauty.

Poets have long realized the power of a pretty face, few more eloquently than Thomas Campion (1567–1620) when he wrote: 'There is a garden in her face/Where roses and white lilies blow.' But what makes a face beautiful? Whether male or female, symmetry is key, so are even, well-placed features, described in the 1930s as 'a good facial contour'. Mathematically, a beautiful face also conforms to the proportions of the 'golden ratio' of 1:1.618, whether it belongs to the Mona Lisa, painted by Leonardo in around 1505, or to any of today's supermodels.

In the days when a dowry was as important as a pretty face, good looks would not necessarily win a man looking for a generous settlement, as in the rhyme:

'Where are you going, my pretty maid?'
'I'm going a-milking, sir,' she said.
'What is your fortune, my pretty maid?'
'My face is my fortune, sir,' she said.
'Then I won't marry you, my pretty maid.'
'Nobody asked you, sir,' she said.

In literature, countless noble women have been immortalized by poets in descriptions of their facial beauty, which is often used as an emblem of their virtues. The radiant beauty of Una, an allegorical figure who represents truth in Edmund Spenser's late 16th-century poem *The Faerie Queen*, is conveyed in cosmic terms:

Her angel's face
As the great eye of heaven, shyned bright,
And made a sunshine in the shady place.

Two centuries later, Sir Walter Scott glorified another allegorical figure, the Arthurian Lady of the Lake, thus:

And ne'er did Grecian chisel trace
A Nymph, a Naiad, or a Grace
Of finer form, or lovelier face!

SHAPED FOR ATTRACTION

The shape of the nose, so the Victorians believed, was a reliable indicator of a person's temperament:

- ROMAN NOSE, WELL ARCHED IN THE CENTRE OR NEAR THE FOREHEAD: born to command.
- GRECIAN OR AQUILINE NOSE: refinement and delicacy combined with a strong will and self-control.
- STRAIGHT NOSE: balanced temperament with equal power to act and suffer.
- TURNED UP OR RETROUSSÉ NOSE: happy disposition and keen sense of humour.

A WARM EMBRACE

Hugging, like kissing, is a form of affection that takes us back to babyhood and onward into the joys of romance. The intimacy of the embrace stimulates the senses as well as the emotions, so that the hug that feels 'just right' can be the prelude to falling in love.

In days gone by, no self-respecting couple would allow themselves to be seen hugging in public, except, perhaps, at the stroke of the New Year or on a girl's doorstep at the end of a date. Such activity was reserved for the cover of darkness. Even in the 1980s, America's Miss Manners raised objections to 'the kind of activity that frightens the horses on the streets'. For men on a first date she advises 'no hugging and kissing' which, she adds, makes it all the more possible to 'act surprised when passion strikes them like lightning'.

IF A GIRL KISSES A MAN WITH A MOUSTACHE, THEN FINDS ONE OF HIS HAIRS REMAINING ON HER LIP THEN, IT'S SAID, SHE WILL DIE A SPINSTER.

The bear hug – a clinch in which the recipient's arms become locked by the side of the body – is named from the behaviour of wild bears when they stand up on their hind legs and use their forearms to immobilize their prey, or when they use all four limbs to hold on to and climb tree trunks. The bunny hug, however, is a kind of dance performed to ragtime rhythm; it was popular in the early years of the 20th century.

A KISS ON THE LIPS

The attraction of the lips lies not just in their shape, but in the power of the kiss as an act of love. As for colour, red lips – like lusciously ripe fruit – have long aroused love's appetites, though lipstick was once regarded as a sinful form of beauty enhancement.

As the lips get thinner with age they become less attractive – hence the popularity of collagen injections to puff them back into youthful beauty.

Helen of Troy was the woman whose beautiful face proverbially 'launched a thousand ships', and a kiss from her lips was equally potent, in the words of the 16th-century dramatist Christopher Marlowe:

> *Sweet Helen, make me immortal with a kiss ...*
> *Here will I dwell for Heaven is in these lips,*
> *And all is dross that is not Helena.*

What makes kissing such a sweet sensation is the fact that the lips are copiously endowed with touch receptors, which respond to the slightest pressure.

ACCORDING TO A 1996 SURVEY BY THE JAPANESE COS-METICS COMPANY SHISEIDO, 87 PER CENT OF AMERICAN WOMEN ADMIT TO HAVING LEFT TRACES OF LIPSTICK IN UNWANTED PLACES — SUCH AS MEN'S COLLARS.

Some evolutionists believe that the kiss is an extension of the mouth-to-nipple contact of babies at the breast, and that it has evolved from the nurturing practice common in the animal world of parents feeding partially digested regurgitated food to their young.

SOME LIPSTICK FACTS

- The ancient Egyptians painted their lips with henna.
- Thomas Hall, a 17th-century English Puritan pastor and the author of the *Loathsomeness of Long Haire* (1653), also wrote a treatise on cosmetics, declaring that face painting was 'the devil's work' and that women who reddened their lips were trying to '... kindle a fire and flame of lust in the hearts of those who cast their eyes upon them'.
- In 1770, the British Parliament passed a law condemning lipstick. Women deemed to have used it to seduce men into matrimony could be tried for witchcraft.
- Lipstick gained respectability in the 1930s, aided by Hollywood and the work of cosmetics pioneers such as Max Factor and Helena Rubenstein.

NAKED AND UNASHAMED

To see one's lover naked is the promise of passion or a first step in the fulfilment of one's desire. But it was not always so. So prudish were many Victorians about their bodies, even those of their spouses, that many shared the experience of John Ruskin, who is said to have fainted in horror on his wedding night.

The glory of nudity began with Adam and Eve. As the Book of Genesis recounts, 'Both were naked, the man and the wife, but they had no feeling of shame.' Only after they had eaten the forbidden fruit did the couple become fearful of their nakedness and try to cover themselves with fig leaves. Before their expulsion from the Garden of Eden they were clothed by God not with fig leaves but in 'garments of skins'.

The ancients had no qualms about viewing or depicting the naked body, nor did the artists of the Renaissance – Michaelangelo's *David* is a sculptured form of supreme beauty, while his painting of the creation of Adam on the ceiling of the Sistine Chapel depicts a beautiful young man clothed only in a minute fig leaf.

In many cultures, nudity has been thought to confer magic powers through the ability of the external sexual organs to ward off evil. According to Pliny, in ancient Rome it was customary for naked virgins to administer a salve made of seven ingredients to cure abscesses while chanting these magic words: 'Apollo says the contagion will not spread where a naked virgin has wiped it out.'

THE SCENT OF A WOMAN – AND A MAN

Since ancient times both men and women have perfumed their bodies to make them attractive to the opposite sex – an aphrodisiac delivered in the form of a fragrance. Coco Chanel believed that a woman should wear perfume wherever she hoped to be kissed.

Marilyn Monroe, the ultimate sex symbol, legendarily declared that all she wore in bed was Chanel No. 5.

In the days before daily baths and showers, perfumes undoubtedly served as much to disguise unpleasant odours as to attract a mate. The ancient Egyptians placed cones of scented fat on their hair, which exuded perfume as they melted. They were the first people to extract perfumes from flowers such as the madonna lily, but the art of distilling scents from flowers such as roses and lavender was not perfected until the 9th century AD in the Middle East.

SOME CLASSIC SCENTS

- EAU DE COLOGNE – manufactured by Giovanni Maria Farina, who settled in Cologne in 1709, using oils of bergamot, neroli, lemon and rosemary. It was popular with soldiers stationed in Cologne during the Seven Years' War.
- CHANEL NO. 5 – launched by Coco Chanel in 1921, it was made exclusively for her by the Russian perfumier Ernest Beaux and given a deliberately 'non-flowery' name. The scent mixes ylang-ylang, neroli, jasmine, rose and sandalwood.
- BLUE GRASS – Elizabeth Arden's long-popular favourite was first sold in 1934.
- VENT VERT – Balmain's 1947 'green breeze'. It was described as 'like a lush meadow blanketed with a rainbow of wildflowers and tender shoots of emerald grass. Green and mossy notes are woven throughout.'

Like other creatures, though to a lesser degree, human bodies produce and are attracted by pheromones – chemicals that influence sexual behaviour. Scientists believe it is the scents produced by the apocrine glands in the armpits that have the most powerful effect. It is a custom in Austrian villages for young girls to dance clenching slices of apple in their armpits, which they then offer to the partners of their choice.

LOVE HURTS

Parting may not always be 'sweet sorrow' as Juliet said to Romeo in Shakespeare's play. The anguish of love may be felt as real pain and it may even be possible to die of a broken heart.

'One must learn to love, and go through a good deal of suffering to get it,' declared the poet and novelist D.H. Lawrence – an experience shared by many a couple. And it is a fact that the trials and tribulations of love, although mental in origin, can indeed be experienced as real pain. Often described by doctors as psychogenic, such pain is commonly accompanied by lethargy and the other symptoms typical of depression.

When two people are truly in love, so scientists have shown, they really can feel each other's pain. Dr Tania Singer, of University College London, believes that this is a kind of empathy in which emotional processes in the brain (not those involved with physical effects) are triggered by the pain of a loved one. For women, the higher their position on the so-called Empathy Scale –

as measured by personality tests – the stronger were their brain responses when their loved ones were given electric shocks.

Many studies show that it is possible to die of a broken heart, especially after the death of a spouse of many years' standing, and the risk of a heart attack is statistically greater in the six months following the death of a spouse, particularly for men. The loss of a soulmate with whom communication was easy and unstressful can make conversation with other people particularly stressful (and raise the blood pressure) after a bereavement.

Thomas Dibdin (1771–1841) penned this melancholy end to his poem 'The Mad Lover's Song':

My wealth is lost, my friend is false,
My love is stolen from me;
And here I lie in misery
Beneath the willow-tree.

LOVE ON THE MIND

Love does peculiar things to the brain, swamping it with feelings that make us absent-minded and forgetful, or worse. It may become an obsession or even, so the superstitious say, have the power to make inanimate objects behave in peculiar ways.

A 1950s schoolgirl could always tell when one of her friends was in love because she'd have the belt of her coat twisted at the back. In earlier times also, clothing was reputed to behave oddly on the infatuated – aprons fell off unbidden and garters untied themselves. And it was a sure sign that a dairymaid was in love if her butter would not 'come' (solidify).

One of the oddest superstitions concerns the plantain, a low-growing wayside plant and lawn weed known in the USA as 'Englishman's foot', with a rosette of leaves that hugs the ground and a club-shaped head from which

---

IF, IT IS SAID, A WOMAN SITTING AT THE TABLE EATING BREAD AND BUTTER ABSENT-MINDEDLY TAKES A SECOND PIECE BEFORE FINISHING THE FIRST, IT IS A SURE SIGN THAT SHE IS IN LOVE.

---

the flowers emerge. Flower heads are picked and put under the clothes, next to the bosom. If your lover is thinking of you the flowers will 'blow', that is, put out stamens.

AFFAIRS OF THE HEART

Falling in love makes the heart beat faster and the blood pressure rise, which means that it is no accident that the heart is the symbol of love and, traditionally, the seat of the emotions, though it did not become the icon of romance until the Middle Ages.

To the ancients, the heart was the centre of all life, and death is still associated with the cessation of the heartbeat. According to the Greek physician Galen (AD 131–201), when the heart expanded during its beat (its diastole), blood became mixed with the *pnuema* or vital spirit from the lungs. He regarded the heart as a furnace, generating the body's heat. William Harvey (1578–1657), who revolutionized medical thinking with his accurate description of the circulation of the blood, was

ABOUT THE BEAT
Things that modern medicine tells us about the heart:

- It is a four-chambered pump, lying to the left side of the chest.
- The heart beats, on average, at around 70 times a minute, during which it pumps about 16 pints of blood.
- When you are excited or afraid the rate can reach 120 or more beats a minute; this can give you the feeling of having 'your heart in your mouth'.
- Although it is the centre of the circulation, the heart has its own blood supply – the coronary arteries.

positively enraptured by the heart's workings: 'To the heart is the beginning of life, the Sun of the Microcosm, as proportionally the Sun deserves to be called the heart of the world … this familiar household god doth his duty to the whole body, by nourishing, cherishing and vegetating, being the foundation of life and author of all.'

FOR ROMAN CATHOLICS, THE 'SACRED HEART', EITHER CROWNED WITH THORNS OR PIERCED WITH NAILS, REPRESENTS THE REDEEMING LOVE OF THE CRUCIFIED AND RESURRECTED CHRIST.

Symbols and Tokens

From the colour red to the arrow through the heart, symbols have been employed for centuries to convey thoughts of love and the promise of a fertile union. Knowing the secret meaning of gifts such as flowers and jewels can give love tokens a special significance.

ARROWS OF DESIRE

The arrows or darts of love are the weapons of the Greek god Eros and his Roman counterpart Cupid. According to myth, no one is immune from the effects of their potent weapons which, when they strike, can induce both love and misery.

Eros, son of Aphrodite, the goddess of love (whose Roman equivalent is Venus), is traditionally portrayed as a pretty young boy armed with a bow and arrow. His body is winged, symbolic of passion's fleeting nature, and he is often depicted carrying a torch – the flame of desire. The Greeks worshipped him as a god of both love and friendship.

Both Eros and Cupid are vain and cruel, but while Eros has the power to transform through love, Cupid's influence is more transient – infatuation rather than lasting love. As the first-century Roman poet Ovid recounted in his *Metamorphoses*, Cupid had two kinds of arrows: one sharp, shining and golden, the other leaden, blunt and heavy. While a hit from the first would inspire its victim with love, the second would bring about fear and repulsion.

Cupid fell in love with Psyche, an earthly maiden so beautiful that she aroused the jealousy of Venus herself. As a result, Venus ordered Cupid to make Psyche fall in love with a vile man. But he disobeyed, carrying her off to a marvellous palace where he visited her at night, without revealing his identity to her. When, contrary to Cupid's instructions, Psyche set eyes on the beautiful boy he punished her by saying that she would never see him again. Hounded by Venus, she searched the world for Cupid. Finally, Jupiter united the lovers by raising Psyche to the status of goddess.

CUPID IS PORTRAYED CARRYING A SHORT BOW WITH A DOUBLE CURVE, AND A CUPID'S BOW IS THE NAME GIVEN TO A MOUTH MADE UP WITH LIPSTICK TO CREATE A SIMILAR SHAPE.

PASSION'S HUE

Red is the colour of the heart, and of the roses given as love symbols, but in folklore red is often associated with ill fate – particularly when it is the colour of a man's hair.

The colour of blood and fire, red is passion's hue. Traditionally it symbolizes the emotions and sexual urges of men and women, and it appears everywhere in love tokens, from the hearts on Valentine cards to red roses. Though lovers have often

written letters to each other in red ink, many regard this as
tempting fate, if not downright unlucky.

Women have been counselled over the centuries to beware of
red-heads. 'It seems generally supposed,' runs an entry in *Notes
& Queries* of 1853 '… that red-haired people are dissemblers,
deceitful, and, in fact, not to be trusted like others whose hair is
of a different colour; and I may add that I myself know persons
who, on that account alone, never admit into their service any
whose hair is thus objectionable.' An earlier warning, of 1654,
says, 'Black-beards are bad, brown dangerous, yellow worse and
red worst of all.'

LOVEBIRDS

**Courting couples bill and coo like lovebirds, and such close
togetherness has many parallels in the animal world – and
not just among birds, though they are the most likely to
form long-term pairings. In medieval Europe, 14 February,
when St Valentine's Day is celebrated, was traditionally the
date when birds were supposed to find their mates.**

Lovebirds, like the popular peach-faced species *Agapornis
roseicollis* kept as household companions all over the world, get
their common name from the way that they constantly preen
each other, a behaviour that is thought to have evolved from the

practical need to keep feathers clean and parasite-free. These small African parrots, coloured bright green with pink faces, also huddle together in pairs, and the male will bring food to his mate while she sits on the eggs and broods her young.

The bond between two lovebirds is so strong that it is not unusual for a single, bereaved caged bird to pine away for lack of companionship. If, however, you want your pet to make a strong bond with you, the advice is to keep just one bird, not a couple. In the wild, lovebirds pair up within the context of a large colony, often taking over the multi-chambered nests of weaver birds.

FROM THE HEART

Even in the age of e-mail, nothing can surpass the handwritten love letter. Whether expressing unrequited passion or infatuation, or reflecting years of married ardour, it is separation that often spurs the deepest emotions.

Inevitably, love letters reflect both the language of the day and lovers' situations. Writing to his mistress Emma Hamilton, just hours before the Battle of Trafalgar in October 1805, Horatio Nelson wrote: 'My dearest beloved Emma, the dear friend of my bosom … May the God of Battles crown my endeavours with success: at all events, I will take care that my name shall ever be most dear to you and Horatia [his illegitimate daughter], both of whom I love as much as my own life …'

The ache of separation is nowhere more intensely expressed than in the poet Dylan Thomas's last letters to his wife Caitlin, written during a reading tour of America a few months before his death in 1953: 'I'm lost without you. I love your body & your soul & your eyes & your hair & your voice & the way you walk & talk.' Pleading for a reply he continues, 'Please if you love me, write to me … Every day's dull torture & every night burning for you.'

THE FRUITS OF LOVE

In the classic fairy tale, Snow White is tempted by the wicked Queen to take a bite from a poisoned apple. She awakes from the death-like slumber it induces only when the Prince kisses her.

The apple is the traditional fruit of temptation between couples, as myth and legend confirm. However, both the fig and the tomato have strong links with the trials and tribulations of romance.

Legend has it that Dionysus, the Greek god of wine and all things pleasurable, created the apple to offer as a gift to Aphrodite, goddess of love. In another myth, the princess

Atalanta declared that she would wed only a man who could outrun her in a race and that all unsuccessful suitors would forfeit their lives. Many tried and failed, then came Milanion, who had gained the protection of Aphrodite, concealing under his tunic three golden apples. Three times during the race Milanion rolled an apple in front of Atalanta, tempting her from her path to pick up the precious fruit – and winning both the victory and the bride.

The tomato, known as the love apple from the French pomme d'amour, *was originally the* pomo dei mori *or 'apple of the Moors'. It was regarded with suspicion as poisonous when first introduced to Britain in the 16th century.*

In the Garden of Eden, the fruit of temptation is most likely to have been a fig, not an apple – the transposition was made by Bible translators unfamiliar with the fruits of the Middle East. And the fig has its own symbolism. Because its shape resembles parts of both male and female sex organs it has long been considered an aphrodisiac.

PURITY AND FERTILITY

Two flowers, the lily and the lotus, have long associations with purity and fruitfulness. Lilies, it is said, will flourish in the garden of a 'good woman'. The lotus is a Hindu symbol of regeneration, female beauty and fertility.

Long before Christians dedicated the white-flowered Madonna lily (*Lilium candidum*) to the Virgin Mary this sweet-scented flower was a symbol of both motherhood and fruitfulness in ancient civilizations. In ancient Greece and Rome the head of a bride would be wreathed with both lilies and corn, since the lily was the flower of Hera, Greek goddess of marriage and childbirth, and of Juno, her Roman equivalent. According to Jewish legend the lily sprang up in the place where Eve shed her tears when, after her expulsion from the Garden of Eden, she discovered that she was pregnant.

Of the many flowers beloved of the ancient Egyptians the lotus was accorded the place of honour. The white lotus or water lily was the flower classified today as *Nymphaea lotus*, but the Egyptians also revered the blue lotus, *N. caerulea*. The sacred flower was believed to be the birthplace of the immortal serpent Nehebkau, who lived in Nun, the primordial ocean that was the source of all life.

The sacred lotus of the Hindus is a different plant, *Nelumbo sp*, a pink-petalled water bean. Brahma, the creator god, is sometimes depicted sitting on a lotus flower, as he is said to have arisen from a 1,000-petalled lotus that grew from the navel of Vishnu, the preserver and a manifestation of the primal deity Brahman. The radiant Lakshmi, wife of Vishnu, is said to be beautiful as a lotus, and is depicted holding the flowers in her hands.

IN YOGA, THE CROSSED-LEGGED LOTUS POSITION IS NAMED FROM THE LEAF OF THE LOTUS TREE; IT IS ASSOCIATED NOT WITH LOVE BUT WITH DETACHMENT.

LIKE A RED, RED ROSE

Roses have been the flowers of love – and secrecy – since, according to myth, Cupid gave a rose to Harpocrates, the god of silence, to prevent him from betraying the secrets of Venus and her love affairs. Red is the colour of the lover's rose because it symbolizes the blood of Adonis, Venus's lover, who was fatally gored by a wild boar.

The role of the rose in legends such as these made it the Romans' favourite flower. Plants were cultivated in vast quantities and their petals were strewn over everything from the floors of banqueting halls to lovers' couches and the graves of the departed. Soldiers returning victorious were garlanded with roses and the flowers were even used to make wine, eaten in rose puddings and celebrated at the festival known as Rosalia.

According to ancient tradition, all roses were originally white but became red when blood was split on them. Basing his story on an ancient Persian tale, Oscar Wilde (1854–1900) recounted the tale of the nightingale who, responding to the desperation of a student searching for the red rose his lover demands, presses her breast on a thorn and sings all night, so that her blood will colour the rose correctly. But there is no happy ending. The girl rejects the flower, insisting that only jewels will satisfy her.

The original rosary, used in prayer, consisted of 165 beads made from dried, rolled rose petals because the rose (white, for purity) was the symbol of the Virgin Mary. To preserve them, some of the beads were covered with lampblack – soot collected from an open-flamed light.

The red rose is immortalized in the verse by the 18th-century Scottish poet Robert Burns:

O, my Luve's like a red red rose
That's newly sprung in June;
O my Luve's like the melodie
That's sweetly played in tune.

SAY IT WITH FLOWERS

The flower posy, which gets it name from 'poesy', the old English word for a love motto or poem, is the perfect symbol of affection. As well as red roses, other flowers in a posy can also reveal lovers' emotions.

Originally a poesy or posy was a saying or verse, such as 'Love is heaven, and heaven is love', 'In thee my choice I do rejoice' or 'Love me and leave me not', inscribed on the inner surface of a ring. That such a gift was often accompanied by a bunch of flowers is probably the reason why a nosegay is called a posy.

But not all blooms will do. The Victorians made great play of the language of flowers, and any girl of the time would have been aware that a posy of daisies would signify fidelity,

marigolds happiness and heliotrope eternal love.
An old-fashioned posy, which the Elizabethans
also called a tussie-mussie, is easy to make and, if
sprinkled with lavender oil and sealed in a paper
bag for a few months, will become permanently
'cured'. Tie the posy with coloured ribbons, chosen
to tone with the flowers and dipped in rose water.

THANKS – AND NO THANKS

**While generosity is an admirable trait, the gifts
exchanged between lovers can have special
significance. Gifts of jewellery, aside from an
engagement ring, are especially acceptable if
they include your lover's birthstone.**

Some gems, however, are believed to have the
power to break love's spell. Mother of pearl is
thought to bring love and luck, and emerald is also
a lucky stone. Opals, however, must be given with

THE STONE OF THE MONTH

Birthstones to give to show true love and their meanings:

Month	Stone(s)	Meaning
JANUARY	garnet	constancy
FEBRUARY	amethyst	sincerity
MARCH	bloodstone, aquamarine	courage
APRIL	diamond, white sapphire	innocence
MAY	emerald	love, success
JUNE	agate, pearl, moonstone	health, longevity
JULY	ruby, carnelian	contentment
AUGUST	sardonyx, peridot	married bliss
SEPTEMBER	sapphire	clear thinking
OCTOBER	opal, tourmaline	hope
NOVEMBER	topaz, citrine	fidelity
DECEMBER	turquoise, zircon	prosperity

The Tiffany pendant – an open heart on a chain – is a popular gift for a girl from the man she loves. Tiffany's was named for Charles F. Tiffany (1812–1902); the name derives from the old custom of giving the name Tiffany to a child born on or around Epiphany (6 January).

care. They have fortunate connotations only for those born in October. Pearls are also unlucky because they are said to bring tears, though it is the custom in Germany to wear them enclosed in a small box or *gegentränen* (an 'averter of tears').

Other gifts that are said to sever love are – for fairly obvious reasons – scissors or knives, but gloves can have the same effect. For all of these it is necessary to pay the giver a token penny or some other small amount in order to render them harmless.

The Gods of Love

The agents of love in the ancient world were the gods and goddesses who were worshipped as the providers of everything from beauty to undying passion. But these figures were often far from benign. Many could wreak violence and vengeance on a whim.

IN THE LAP OF THE GODS

For the earliest civilizations, love was represented by the gentler aspects of the great mother goddesses. But these complex deities could also be wrathful and treacherous.

Ishtar, the Babylonian goddess of love and fertility and the protector of harlots, was much feared because all those whom she took as lovers she destroyed. She was also goddess of war and, like the gods Eros and Cupid, she was armed with a bow and arrow.

In praise of Aphrodite, Homer eulogized 'the beauty of her neck and her lovely breasts and sparkling eyes'.

Hathor, the Egyptian goddess often portrayed as a woman with the head of a cow, or with a cow's horns and a sun disc on her head, is an early love goddess and typically contrary in nature. As a beautiful woman she celebrated the joy of life and love, but she also had a destructive aspect as a divine lioness.

In Hindu mythology, the milkmaid Radha and her lover Krishna are the deifications of true love. Radha was the wife of the cowherd Ayanagosha. Ayanagosha, tipped off by his sister, went in search of his wife with her lover but found her instead worshipping a goddess – Krishna in disguise.

LANGUAGE OF THE GODS

Music has, since its invention, had the power to arouse all the emotions and appetites. In mythology it even allowed Orpheus to recover his love from the underworld.

When he sang and played the lyre even the animals and birds were entranced by Orpheus, the son of Apollo (himself the god of music, poetry and prophecy) and Calliope, the poetic muse. After the death of his wife Eurydice from a snakebite, Orpheus descended into the underworld, where his playing and singing were so passionate that even the iron-souled Hades, ruler of the kingdom of death, was moved to tears.

Eurydice was released, but on the condition that Orpheus leave the underworld without looking back at her until he reached the earth's surface. Unfortunately the story had no happy ending, for just as they were emerging into the light, Orpheus forgot Hades' stricture and glanced back, condemning himself and his wife to permanent separation. He wandered the world playing his lyre and, say some accounts, was killed by a group of Thracian women infuriated by his undying love for his wife.

The lyre favoured by Orpheus was an early stringed instrument known from ancient times. In the Old Testament there are numerous references to the harp – probably the Hebrew lyre, which was used only to play joyful music – and to the psaltery, which consisted of strings stretched over a flat box with four unequal sides. The strings were plucked with quills or the fingers.

THE LOVE GODDESS

Aphrodite was the Greek goddess of love, beauty and fertility, whose powerful cult later became identified with the Roman goddess Venus. Aphrodite's name means 'born of the sea foam', and she was said to have arisen, fully formed, from the ocean.

Legend has it that the beautiful Aphrodite made her entrance to the world from waters dyed red with the blood of battle and was saved from drowning by a seashell. As she stood on the shell, the drops of water that fell from her body landed in the shell as pearls. Entranced by her beauty, Zephyrus, the god of the west wind, blew the shell to the island of Cyprus. As she touched land, flowers sprang up at her feet and a bevy of beautiful maidens came to greet her and escort her to the home of the gods.

Every god on Mount Olympus desired Aphrodite for his wife, but she rejected them all. As a punishment, Zeus gave her in marriage to the lame, gauche Hephaestus, god of fire. Aphrodite was unfaithful to her husband, taking Ares, the war god, as her lover, to whom she bore twin sons, Deimos (fear) and Phobos (panic). However, her true love was for the beautiful youth Adonis, despite having to share him with Persephone, queen of the dead.

As love goddesses entrap the men who take their fancy, so the carnivorous plant the Venus flytrap (Dionaea muscipula) devours insects. When 'prey' lands on one of its hinged leaves this quickly snaps shut. Over the ensuing ten days or so the insect is digested by the plant, providing it with essential nutrients.

In art, the goddess is best known in her Roman form, Venus, in works such as Botticelli's painting of around 1483, *The Birth of Venus*, and the *Venus de Milo,* the classical Greek sculpture created in the 2nd century BC and discovered, minus its arms, on the Greek island of Melos in 1820. It is now in the Louvre in Paris.

THE BEAUTIFUL BOY

Young men with flawless looks who are adored by women are still given the tag Adonis, after the young lover of Aphrodite (Venus). Because plants bloomed in his path, and from the tragic circumstances of his death, he has also lent his name to various flowers.

Of all the youths beloved of Aphrodite, Adonis was the most handsome. He was born from the incestuous union of Theias, king of Assyria, and his daughter Myrrha, who was compelled by Aphrodite to trick her father into sleeping with her. When he discovered that she was pregnant he tried to kill her, and the gods turned her into a tree for her protection. Adonis was delivered when a boar's tusk pierced the tree and was so beautiful that Aphrodite hid him in a casket, which she gave to Persephone, goddess of the underworld, for safekeeping. When she came back to claim her 'treasure' Aphrodite discovered that the casket had been opened and that Persephone had decided to keep the baby for herself.

SEVERAL FLOWERS OF THE BUTTERCUP FAMILY ARE GIVEN THE NAME *ADONIS*, BUT BEST KNOWN IS THE ANEMONE-LIKE RED-FLOWERED PHEASANT'S EYE, *ADONIS ANNUA*.

To settle the dispute between the goddesses, Zeus commanded that Adonis should spend half of each year with Persephone and the other half with Aphrodite. While he was in the underworld the world was barren and infertile, but it sprang to life as he returned 'above ground' each spring.

Adonis met his end when charged by a wild boar. Aphrodite, overcome with grief, turned his spilt blood into flowers, as an ancient Greek poet described:

As many drops as from Adonis bled,
So many tears the sorrowing
  Aphrodite shed:
For every drop on earth a flower
  there grows:
Anemones for tears; for blood
  the rose.

Adonis, meaning 'lord', was the name originally given to the dying-and-rising Babylonian god Tammuz, whose cult moved westward into ancient Greece.

Love's Seasons

Any day of the year is good for falling in love but there are many occasions, such as on St Valentine's Day, when boy and girl may meet in especially propitious circumstances. Most, like kissing under the mistletoe, are linked to the rituals of the passing seasons.

At Midsummer a girl would pick a rose, keep it wrapped in paper, then wear it on Christmas Day. To reveal himself, her lover would take the flower from her.

LOVE'S CALENDAR

Most probably because of their ancient link with the monthly female cycle of fertility, the phases of the moon have long been connected with falling in love. The year's round of festivals made good excuses for partying and were, in times of all-consuming work, prime opportunities for meeting your life's partner – or at least enjoying a night of pleasure.

On the night of a new moon you can, it is said, dream of the person you're to marry. To do so you should, before bed, fold your hands across your chest and say three times: 'New moon, new moon, I pray thee tell me this night who my true love will be.' You must then go to bed without speaking to anyone. Alternatively you can go outside and ask the moon the same question direct.

St Valentine's Day falls either before or during Lent, and it was not until Easter that girls traditionally paraded in their new clothes and, of course, bonnets.

With spring comes the rising of the sap in plants and, by tradition, of young men's desires. As well as being attractive to the opposite sex, the new clothes girls wore at Easter were said to bring good luck.

Many seasonal courtship rituals are linked to the annual cycle of farming and the fertility of crops.

BE MY VALENTINE

The red heart, possibly pierced with an arrow, is the symbol of love, and to lose your love is to suffer from a broken heart. St Valentine's Day, 14 February, is the occasion for hearts and flowers – but anonymity is the rule.

In ancient Rome, February, the start of the 'mating season', was the month of the festival of Lupercalia, when virile young men, clad only in strips from the skins of sacrificial goats, ran around the city's ancient boundary to purify it. As they ran they also lashed out, with further goatskin strips, at the women in the gathered crowd – being hit in this way was thought to be a guarantee of fertility.

IT IS AN OLD COUNTRY SAYING THAT IF A YOUNG WOMAN LOOKS THROUGH HER KEYHOLE ON ST VALENTINE'S MORNING AND SEES A COCK AND HEN TOGETHER, SHE WILL BE SURE TO HAVE A SWEETHEART.

From the word meaning 'to purify', *februare*, came the name of the month. When the Christians adopted the Roman festival, they attributed it to St Valentine – whether a specific one, or to both the St Valentines with feast days on the 14th of the month, we do not know.

The sending of Valentine cards is believed to have been started by Charles, duc d'Orleans, when he was imprisoned in the Tower of London after the Battle of Agincourt in 1415. When sending Valentine cards caught on, the first ones were handwritten and hand-delivered – and often handmade. By the late 19th century they came in all manner of embossed, padded and lacy forms – some even had moving parts or 'mechanicals' incorporated into them. They often contained riddles for the recipient to solve – and so discover the identity of the sender.

LEAP YEAR

Convention becomes turned on its head on 29 February, when a woman may propose to her sweetheart. Even if he rejects her advances, this is not always the end of the story.

Every four years, in leap or ladies' year, girls have their day. It was once their right, if their proposal was rejected, to claim the compensation of a silk gown or a pay-off. An ordinance of the Scottish Parliament of 1288 laid down the rules of engagement. Translated into modern English it reads, '… for each year known as leap year, old maiden ladies of both high and low estate shall have liberty to bespeak the man she likes, albeit he refuses to take her to be his lawful wife, he shall be mulcted [fined] the sum of one pound or less, as his estate may be.' If the man could prove that he was already betrothed to another woman, then he was totally free.

In the modern Gregorian calendar, which began on 15 October 1582, a leap year occurs when the last two digits of the year are divisible by four, but to keep the calendar in synch with the solar year, the first year of a century is only a leap year if the whole date is divisible by 400. So 2000 was a leap year but 1900 was not.

A Devon newspaper, *The Ilfracombe Chronicle* of 1 June 1872, reported the extraordinary tale of a Mr Rogers, a retired baker from Stafford of 'unassuming and almost retiring manners', who had been proposed to by a 'maiden lady of fabulous wealth'. He refused her, but within two weeks the woman was dead. In her will she bequeathed the lucky Mr Rogers her entire fortune, which included 'a large estate in Cumberland, a mansion in Belgravia, picture galleries, horses, broughams and a suit of servants'.

QUEEN OF THE MAY

On May Day, 1 May, the fairest maid of the town or village was crowned Queen of the May in a celebration whose origins date back to Roman fertility rites. This is still a day for dancing – especially around the maypole.

On the Calends, or first day of May in Roman times, young men would go out into the fields and dance and sing in honour of Flora, the goddess of flowers and fruits. The practice of 'going a-Maying' persisted, and in Europe the hawthorn, or may flower, and the rowan tree became popular fertility symbols. It was probably these trees that were originally danced around, though as the maypole evolved, birch, elm or pine were substituted.

The fetching of the maypole on May Day eve was another occasion for young men and women to indulge their fancies. In his *Anatomie of Abuses* (1583) the Puritan Philip Stubbes condemned such behaviour: 'I have heard it credibly reported … that of forty, three score or a hundred maids going to the wood overnight there have scarcely the third part of them returned home again undefiled.'

The decoration of the maypole – and of homes – with foliage and flowers was a means of ensuring the fertility of the coming seasons. As well as the communal maypole individual ones were set up in front of people's homes as symbols of love for sweethearts and of fertility for young couples.

MORRIS DANCING AND THE LIGHTING OF BONFIRES ARE OTHER MAY DAY TRADITIONS. IN THE LEGEND OF ROBIN HOOD THE OUTLAW AND HIS MAID MARIAN PRESIDED AS LORD AND LADY OF THE MAY, AND IN MANY PLACES IN ENGLAND IN THE 16TH CENTURY, MAY DAY WAS KNOWN AS ROBIN HOOD'S DAY.

In these lines from his 'Song on May Morning' the poet John Milton celebrated the season of love:
Hail bounteous May that dost inspire
Mirth and youth, and warm desire;
Woods and Groves, are of thy dressing,
Hill and Dale, doth boast thy blessing.

SUMMER LOVING

From *A Room With a View* to *Grease*, holiday romances have been the stuff of fiction and film, but they also happen a million times over in real life. And it is no accident that couples have success in conceiving children while they are on holiday.

In days past, summer activities – from bringing in the harvest to picnicking in the fields – were ideal opportunities for romance for country folk. For young townspeople, pulses would race at gatherings in fashionable country towns such as Bath, Vichy and Baden Baden, visited for their health-giving waters. From the end of the 19th century, the beach, the seaside hotel, the country house and the holiday camp all became popular holiday destinations. And the vogue for cycling that mushroomed in the 1890s gave young women the chance for exciting – unchaperoned – summer expeditions.

Cruise ships, popular long before the days of airline travel, are also ideal venues for burgeoning holiday romance, though the small space and claustrophobic conditions are not ideal if holiday love goes wrong. The first long-haul holidays were provided by Thomas Cook, who also pioneered the package holiday, though his educational excursions down the Rhine were a far cry from today's all-night clubbing at package resorts on Ibiza.

Whether love took the form of a 'roll in the hay' or merely a daring kiss on the hand or a grasp of the arm, the baring of flesh that became

ONE REASON THAT BABIES ARE OFTEN CONCEIVED ON HOLIDAY IS BELIEVED TO BE THAT VITAMIN D, THE VITAMIN PRODUCED BY THE BODY IN SUNLIGHT, HAS AN ADVANTAGEOUS EFFECT ON THE HEALTH OF A MAN'S SPERM AND THE QUANTITY PRODUCED.

fashionable from the 1920s, along with the vogue for a suntan that would previously have been viewed with horror, rapidly became a means of allure, from the very act of lying on the beach or sunlounger to the mask-like mystery of sunglasses.

LOVE AT HALLOWEEN

As well as being the day of commemoration of the departed, All Hallows' Eve on 31 October is the night on which fortune telling turns its attention to love. To assist in divination, seasonal fruits and plants are regularly employed.

The coming together of the natural and the supernatural is what gives Halloween its power to foretell – or possibly influence – the future of love. Typical is the 'ceremony' of roasting chestnuts. As they are put into the fire, two chestnuts are 'named'

SEEING YOUR LOVE

Many of the love superstitions of Halloween, like the nuts and cabbages, were included by Robert Burns in a poem published in 1786. Others are:

* Eat an apple in front of a mirror lit by candlelight and comb your hair as you do so. You will see your lover's face peering over your shoulder.
* Go out into a field without being seen and sow a handful of hemp seed. Then chant 'Hemp seed I sow thee, hemp seed I sow thee; and he [or she] that be my true love come after me.' Look over your left shoulder and you will see a vision of your love pulling up the grown hemp.
* Unseen, go into the barn but leave the doors open. Take the winnowing sieve and throw the corn into the wind three times. On the third attempt, you will see your lover come in by one door and leave by the other.

after two young people. If the nuts roast steadily side by side then the pair will marry and be happy. But a less propitious fate awaits them if either or both nuts jump away from each other or burst.

To 'see' their future spouse on Halloween, young men would pull up cabbages. Depending on whether the root was large or small, and whether covered with clinging earth or clean, a future wife would be tall or short, rich or poor respectively. Girls would do the same, and they would also put a veil over the mirror until midnight. When it was removed, their true loves' faces would appear.

That yearly Halloween celebrations involve customs such as 'bobbing' for apples relates to the Roman worship of Pomona, the goddess of fruit trees, whose festival was held in late autumn.

A CHRISTMAS KISS

Kisses stolen under the mistletoe can, by tradition, be claimed back later in the year, as long as a berry is plucked at Christmas time and is later produced on demand. The plant, with its paired, splayed leaves between which the shining white berries nestle, has long been a symbol of fertility.

Hanging up mistletoe at Christmas – or placing it around the necks of children – was originally a means of keeping witches and other evil spirits at bay and, in medieval times, was thought to have the power to cure illnesses and even end epileptic fits. The plant's long association with fertility may relate to the fact that it grows so prolifically on apple trees, but it was the revival of interest in the Druids (for whom the mistletoe was linked with human sacrifice) and their customs that cemented the link.

Both men and women may pick mistletoe berries. A man would pluck one berry for each kiss, keeping them for future encounters. For women, *Yorkshire Customs* of 1898 recounts a practice that involved both holly and mistletoe: 'Some maiden

In Scandinavia, the mistletoe is ceremonially gathered at Midsummer, not at Christmas, and is considered a plant of peace, under which enemies are reconciled.

mayhap has retired to her chamber with a leaf and a berry plucked from the mistletoe under which she has been saluted. Having locked her door, the berry must be swallowed, whilst on the leaf she will prick the initials of him her heart loves best; this she will stitch in the inside of her corset, so that it rest near her heart, and thus bind his love to her so long as there it remains.'

THE MISTLETOE (*VISCUM ALBUM*) IS A PARASITIC PLANT THAT GROWS, AS WELL AS ON APPLES, ON POPLARS, WILLOWS AND OTHER TREES. THE DRUIDS PARTICULARLY PRIZED MISTLETOE GROWING ON OAK TREES.

Famous Lovers

The annals of both history and fiction are amply provided with names that have entered, and remained in, the all-time register of love. Even though their stories often ended in tragedy, their names live on in popular culture as epitomes of passion.

THE LATIN LOVER

It may have started with Casanova – or Romeo – but Hollywood was the birthplace of the screen's great Latin lovers, starting with the proverbial heart-throb Rudolph Valentino.

When he died in 1926, at the age of just 31, Valentino was mourned by thousands of women: it was said that 100,000 tried to attend his funeral, leading to riots on the streets of New York, and so great was their grief that some even committed suicide. He was possessed of huge, 'almost occult' eyes, with which he glared 'until the vast areas of white [were] visible', and habitually flared his nostrils and drew back 'the lips of his wide, sensuous mouth to bare his gleaming teeth'.

Born Rodolfo d'Antonguolla in 1895 in Italy, Valentino arrived in New York on 23 December 1913, where he took on a variety of jobs. While he was working as a busboy in an Italian restaurant, an older waiter took Rudolph under his wing and taught him to dance. Soon the tango became his speciality and he was supplementing his income by working as a gigolo. This afforded him an invaluable opportunity to study the desires and fantasies of women and to perfect the art of seduction.

At the height of his fame, in 1921, Valentino was cast in the coveted role of Julio in *The Four Horsemen of the Apocalypse*. His graceful dance moves and sexual allure lit up the screen and with his role in *The Sheik* his Latin lover stardom was secured.

On 14 August 1926 Valentino attended an all-night party in his honour. The next day he was found writhing on the floor in agony. He was rushed to hospital and operated on for a perforated gastric ulcer, but complications set in and he died nine days later.

THE MOVIE CONTENDERS

There are some other worthy candidates for the title of great screen lover:

- RAMON NAVARRO, the brooding Mexican actor who played Rupert in *The Prisoner of Zenda* (1922).
- CESAR ROMERO, matinée idol and star of *The Gay Caballero* (1940).
- The smouldering French actor LOUIS JOURDAN, whose screen debut was in *Le Corsaire* (1939).
- TYRONE POWER, who made his name in *Jesse James* (1939) and *The Mark of Zorro* (1940).
- CLARK GABLE, irresistible as Rhett Butler in *Gone with the Wind* (1939).

THE GREAT LOVER

Most notorious of all the Latin lovers was Casanova, the 18th-century Venetian womanizer – who was also a writer, trickster, soldier and musician. His many encounters with women are recorded in his lengthy _Mémoires_.

Giovanni Giacomo Casanova was born in Venice in 1725. Imprisoned in 1755, accused of conducting magic and of being a Freemason, he subsequently escaped and travelled around Europe, consorting with the great and the good and styling himself the Chevalier de Seingalt. He also swindled many, claiming to have occult powers. Among his victims was the 'divine madwoman' Mme la Marquise d'Urfé, an ageing Parisienne who wanted to be 'reborn' as a man.

Casanova was dedicated to the pursuit of pleasure in its many forms. To be sure of sustenance at all times while on the move he habitually carried concentrated 'pocket' or tablet soup with him, rather like today's concentrated stock cubes.

In his travels Casanova encountered such dignitaries as Catherine the Great of Russia, Pope Clement XIII, Voltaire and Frederick the Great. Among his explanations for his problems – including exile and further imprisonment – were his self-confessed susceptibility to the 'allurements of all forms of sensual delight'. The cultivation of such pleasures, he confessed, 'was my principle concern throughout my life'. However, he also commented, 'I do not know whether it was by my intellect that I have come so far in life, I do know that it is to it alone that I owe all the happiness I enjoy when I am face to face with myself.'

IN LONDON IN SUMMER, CASANOVA WOULD FREQUENT THE VAUXHALL GARDENS WHERE, AS WELL AS MUSICAL ENTERTAINMENT, WOMEN WERE FREELY AVAILABLE (NOT NECESSARILY LITERALLY). HE DID NOT ALWAYS MAKE A CATCH FOR, AS HE HIMSELF RELATES, HE 'OFFERED [A WOMAN] TWO GUINEAS IF SHE WOULD COME AND TAKE A LITTLE WALK WITH ME IN A DARK ALLEY'. BUT, HAVING TAKEN HIS MONEY, SHE FLED.

WHEREFORE ART THOU ROMEO?

Of all fictional lovers, Romeo and Juliet are surely the best known. Today a 'Romeo' is not just a lover but a true romantic, staking all against the odds in the fashion of his namesake, whose romance was thwarted by the enmity between the Montagues and the Capulets.

Shakespeare took his plot from a poem written by Arthur Brooke in 1562, itself based on a story of 1535 by one Luigi da Porto.

Some of Shakespeare's most memorable scenes and lines are acted out in the tragic romance of *Romeo and Juliet*. Romeo is totally overcome when he sees his love at her window (in the scene traditionally played on a balcony) as morning approaches. Like any modern man, Romeo has to work hard to prove his love. Though Juliet confesses that 'In truth fair Montague, I am too fond,' he still has to answer her question 'Dost thou love me?' and despite his swearing 'by yonder blessed moon' she is not satisfied until she receives the promise of 'the exchange of thy love's faithful vow for mine'.

Tragedy befalls the star-crossed lovers when, after they are secretly married, Romeo kills the Capulet Tybalt, Juliet's cousin, and is banished from Verona. Juliet's father compels her to agree to marry Paris, the man he has chosen for her, and to avoid this predicament she is drugged into a death-like trance with the help of her priest. But the plan misfires and Romeo receives no word of the deception. He returns to Verona and, finding her apparently lifeless, takes poison. Juliet awakes to find him dead, takes his dagger and kills herself. The tragedy ends the feud between the lovers' families.

The Romeo and Juliet tale has been retold in many forms over the years. The musical West Side Story, about rival New York gangs the Sharks and the Jets, was an instant hit when it opened on Broadway in October 1957.

THEY BECAME PRINCESSES

The brides and princesses of fairy tales are all, of course, endowed with great beauty, though this is not necessarily recognized at the time. Equally, they are all forced to suffer greatly before they find their happy endings.

The contrast between heroines of noble and lowly birth is typified by the difference between Snow White who, even when only seven years old, has a complexion 'as clear as the noon day' and is 'more beautiful than the [wicked] Queen', and Cinderella, whose beauty is marred by dirt and cinders (hence her nickname) and revealed only when she is magically transformed, complete with glittering dress and golden slippers, to go to the ball where she is to meet her prince.

At Snow White's wedding, so the story goes, the Queen was forced to dance in a pair of iron shoes, heated in the fire until red hot, until she dropped down dead.

Snow White, poisoned by a bite from the apple brought to her by the queen disguised as an old woman, is reverently placed in a glass casket by the adoring dwarfs who have befriended her, until a prince sees her and falls in love with her. Reluctantly the dwarfs allow him to take her away. As he kisses her the apple lodged in her throat comes free and she awakes.

Cinderella's tormentors are her ugly stepsisters. When the prince comes looking for the girl whose foot will fit the slipper discarded in her midnight dash from the ball, even her father is reluctant to allow her to be seen. But the 'baddies' get their deserts – the ugly sisters are smitten with blindness as a punishment for their wickedness.

CINDERELLA'S MODERN INCARNATION IS PRINCESS MIA, HEROINE OF MEG CABOT'S BESTSELLER *THE PRINCESS DIARIES*. THIS FRUMPY DAUGHTER OF A SINGLE MOTHER HAS HER LIFE TRANSFORMED BY THE QUEEN OF GENOVIA, WHO TRAINS HER UP TO RULE IN HER PLACE.

SOME DAY MY PRINCE WILL COME

In her dreams of love, many a girl will long for a handsome prince to come and sweep her off her feet, rescue her from her mundane or tormented existence and live with her happily ever after. But in every fairy tale there are evil forces that must somehow be overcome before the love match can take place.

The prince of fairy tales finds his bride in many different guises, but the common thread that runs through most of the stories is that the girl is good – and beautiful – but hampered by being either poor or ill-treated, or both. Whether having to endure being transformed into a frog, cutting through thickets or climbing high towers, the

Pretty Woman, starring Julia Roberts and Richard Gere, is the 1990 movie version of the Cinderella 'rags to riches' story.

prince has to prove himself, like the heroes of ancient legend. Meanwhile witches, wicked queens and their ilk are laying traps along his way.

Typical is the story of Rapunzel, the girl with the extravagantly long hair, shut up in a tower by a wicked witch. When her prince finds her he calls up to her, as he has heard the witch do, 'Rapunzel, Rapunzel, let down your hair,' and uses the girl's tresses to climb the tower. However, one day he finds that he has been tricked by the witch, who has discovered what has been

MORE TALES OF PRINCELY LOVE

- Sleeping Beauty is awakened by a kiss from a prince, but only after he has cut his way through a dense entanglement of thorns.
- The Frog Prince is returned to mortal form by a kiss from his love, the beautiful princess.
- In the tale of the Goose Girl the prince has to endure marriage to a false bride before the identity of his princess is revealed.
- Taking in a poor girl caught in a storm, a lonely prince – who has travelled the world looking for a suitable bride – proves that she is a true princess by having her sleep on a pile of mattresses under which she is able to feel a single pea.

happening, cut off Rapunzel's hair and banished her. The witch pushes the prince off the tower and he falls into a thorn thicket. Blind and wounded, he wanders the world for years, but is finally reunited with his beloved, who cures his blindness with two of her tears.

ROUES, CADS AND BOUNDERS

Men with the reputation for being 'fast and loose' have always had an irresistible attraction for some women, becoming the object of their infatuation, if not their love. These are the world's most infamous love rats, who renege on their promises to women and men alike and behave in a generally despicable fashion.

The term 'cad' derives from 'cadet' – historically a younger son or brother who was sent away to be trained as an army officer. The modern cad is a character such as the late Princess Diana's lover James Hewitt who, after her death, sold his story to the tabloid press for £1 million and was, in July 2004, arrested for possessing cocaine. As one Buckingham Palace confidant is said to have commented, 'Once a cad, always a cad.'

The original roué was the dissipated debauchee Philippe, duc d'Orléans, Regent of France from 1715 to 1723. His boast was that he and his companions deserved no better fate than to be 'broken on the wheel', a form of execution in France reserved for crimes of especial atrocity (*roue* is French for 'wheel').

THE DEROGATORY TERM 'BOUNDER' MAY RELATE TO THE HABITUAL BEHAVIOUR OF DOGS. SO, LOGICALLY, A MAN WHO BEHAVES LIKE A DOG, OR CUR, DESERVES TO BE NAMED AFTER ONE.

Who'll be my Love?

From the moment the hormones of puberty begin to take effect, the urge for love grows stronger. The practice of conjuring up lovers' forms, forecasting their occupations or guessing their innermost thoughts, has for centuries been a light-hearted way of relieving the tension while waiting for true love to strike.

PREDICTING LOVE

From counting cherry stones on the plate rim to interpreting the patterns of tea leaves or coffee grounds, there are dozens of ways in which young people wanting to be in love have tried to divine the shape or occupation of their partner-to-be. That these have no relation to the truth is not the point!

'Tinker, tailor, soldier, sailor, rich man, poor man, beggarman ... thief' – so runs the well-known rhyme for predicting a husband's occupation from the number of fruit stones left on the plate. An old outdoor alternative, once popular in the country, is for a girl to dig a hole in the ground at a place where three roads meet. She then bends down and puts her ear to it, expecting to hear, in a whisper, the trade of her future lover.

To single out one boy or girl from a group, knife spinning is another ruse. The boys (or girls) sit in a

---

THE FIRST-EVER KNIVES WERE MADE OF SHELLS, FLINTS OR BONES. NEOLITHIC CRAFTSMEN SKILFULLY CHIPPED THE EDGES OF FLINTS TO RAZOR SHARPNESS AND SLOTTED THEM INTO WOODEN HANDLES.

---

ring and each girl (or boy) spins a knife. Whoever it points to when it stops spinning is the partner for you. As to the shape or character of one's lover-to-be, this could be divined from the look of a cabbage stalk pulled up on Halloween. A club root indicated a club foot, a crooked stalk a mean old man, and a well-grown one a handsome lover.

> *To marry a rich man, you should have on your body 'three moles within a span', that is within the distance covered by your outstretched hand. But two moles on a woman's cheek signifies two husbands.*

LOVE'S PRELUDE

As well as dreaming of her love there are, in folk tradition, dozens of ways for a girl to make him appear – as well as actions reputed to ensure a meeting with her husband-to-be.

Numbers are significant here – and sometimes long-term counting is necessary. In the days when reverend gentlemen were more numerous than today it was said that after seeing 100 clergymen the next man you set eyes on would be your future husband. A two-leaved clover, put in the right shoe, would have the same effect.

The number nine was also important. In the hope of their love crossing the threshold, girls would hang a perfect nine-pea pod over the door. More rigorous was the sword and scabbard routine, as described in *Mother Bunch's Closet* of 1885: 'You dare venture yourselves into a church-yard just as it strikes twelve, take there a naked sword in your hand and go nine times about the church, saying only thus, "Here's the sword, but where's the scabbard?" and the ninth time the person you are to marry

> *Nine is thought to be important to love rituals because a baby's gestation period in the womb is nine months.*

will meet you with the scabbard and kiss you.' Other ways to conjure a meeting with your love include washing your face in May dew (which will of course do wonders for the complexion), seeing a heart-shaped cinder spit from an open fire, or finding – and holding in your hand – an ash leaf with an even number of leaflets.

WHAT'S THE NAME?

Even if love is not on the horizon, it is fun to try finding out what the initial of your future husband or wife may be. By tradition it is possible to use anything from apple peel to a snail's trail for such predictions.

First peel your apple – making sure that the peel is all in one piece. Then, as instructed in the *Everlasting Fortune Teller* of 1839, hold the peel in your right hand and say, 'St Simon and St Jude, on you I intrude,/By this paring I hold to discover,/Without any delay, to tell me this day,/The first letter of my own true-lover.' You must then turn around three times and throw the peel over your left shoulder. When it lands it will form the initial. If, instead, a girl hangs the peel behind the front door, the next man to enter the house will have the same first name as the person she will marry.

There are other ways of learning the initial letter. You can prick an egg and let the white drop into hot water, creating a letter as it sets, or, before

Women have long been cautioned to take care, when choosing a husband, that he has a lucky surname. For, as the old saying goes: 'Change the name and not the letter, change for worse and not for better.'

> *A snail trail is the dried remains of the lubricating fluid it secretes to aid its movement.*

you go to bed at night, put a snail on a dinner plate or into a box. In the morning you will find the initial of your lover-in-waiting. You can also chant the alphabet while twisting the stalk from an apple – the significant letter is the one that coincides with the moment it breaks off. Or if your ears start ringing, chant the alphabet and see which letter you've reached when the ringing stops.

Yet another method is to write each letter of the alphabet on a separate piece of paper, and put them in a bowl of water overnight. In the morning, the initial of a future spouse will be the one that has turned over.

HE LOVES ME ... HE LOVES ME NOT

If your cheek tingles for no reason, your love is thinking about you. So the old saying goes, but can we really tell whether our love is true?

Only time will give the ultimate answer, but countless lovelorn girls and young men have sat and pulled the petals off a daisy, chanting 'He loves me, he loves me not' or 'She loves me, she loves me not'. The answer comes with the removal of the last petal. Or the final petal can settle the answer to one of these questions: 'Does he love me – much – a little – devotedly – not at all?'

Apple pips are also useful in such divination, especially at times of indecision. The way to resolve the issue is to take two apple pips, and give each the name of a suitor. The pips must then be pressed one on each cheek or both on to the forehead. Whichever pip sticks the longest determines the true lover.

A dandelion 'clock' or seedhead can work in a similar way to a daisy. As you blow the seeds – preferably towards the home of your desired one – chant 'Love me, love me not,' or 'Does he love me? Yes, No, Yes, No.' The last puff will provide the answer. It is especially lucky if just one seed is left before the final breath. That means your love is thinking of you.

> *Love and daisies have an ancient association, and young girls have for centuries adorned their heads and necks with daisy chains.*

FROM WHERE – AND WHEN?

> *Ladybirds (ladybugs), who fly away when you hold them on your hand, have inspired a number of rhymes. As the insect takes to the air you can say: 'Up your wings and fly away,/Over land and over sea,/Tell me where my love can be.' Or 'Marygold, Marygold, flitter to fly,/Tell me where doth my lady-love lie?'*

The unwed wishing to meet the right life partner can use the signs of nature to divine how long they will have to wait for love to come their way – and from which direction. And there are even signs to be read from the behaviour of everyday objects.

When you hear the first cuckoo of spring, count the number of calls: that's the number of years until you marry. Or the years you have to wait can be counted by the number of puffs it takes to clear a dandelion clock. Apple pips can again be put to good use. You hold a pip between finger and thumb then shoot it out, saying: 'Kernel come kernel, hop over my thumb,/And tell me which way my truelove will come,/East, west, north or south,/Kernel jump into my truelove's mouth.'

To find out if you will be married within the year, rituals can be performed at Halloween and on Midsummer's Eve – auspicious days for fortune telling. Typical is the Irish custom in which three things are placed on the table: a piece of turf, a bowl of water and a ring. A young man or woman is led into the room blindfold. Whoever touches the ring will be married within the year. (But woe betide anyone who doesn't choose correctly: those who touch the turf will die, while those who touch the water are said to be doomed to drown within the twelvemonth.)

LOVE'S YOUNG DREAM

'In dreams and love,' so the proverb goes, 'nothing is impossible.' It is supremely pleasurable to dream of true love, but nowadays it would take some desperation to go to the great lengths taken by young men and women in times past.

Putting something 'potent' under your pillow is a long-established way to induce a dream of your lover. With their obvious connections with both romance and fertility, pieces of wedding or christening cake are believed to be especially effective, as are other edibles, including so-called 'groaning'

SWEET DREAMS

How to make your lover come to you in a dream:

- Put lemon peel under your pillow – but first keep it in your armpit all day.
- Arrange your shoes in a T shape beside your bed.
- On a Friday night, put your left stocking inside your right and tie them around your neck.
- Peel an onion, wrap it in a handkerchief, and put it under your head. This is specially effective on St Thomas's Eve (20 December) and St Martin's Eve (10 November).
- Put a pigeon's heart stuck with pins under your pillow.

---

cakes and cheeses, which were traditionally made to celebrate a woman's successful confinement and the birth of a baby.

To conjure up the image of your love, another age-old method is to eat salt herrings before bed, or a hard-boiled egg in which the yolk has been replaced with salt. Not only will you see your partner-to-be in your dreams but he or she will bring you the water you need to quench your raging thirst.

Some days in the year are particularly auspicious for love's apparition. If you go to bed without supper on St Agnes Eve, 20 January, then you will dream of your love. On the night of a new moon, cross your hands over your chest and say three times: 'New moon, new moon, I pray thee, tell me this night who my true love will be.' Your dream will answer the question.

LUCKY – AND UNLUCKY – IN LOVE

Unlucky at cards, lucky in love, so the old proverb goes. And, it is said, love lasts only as long as money endures. In the days when divorce was not only uncommon but a social taboo, it was especially important to fall in love with the right person – or have them chosen for you in an arranged marriage.

When it was the custom to wear black mourning clothes for months after the death of a loved one, it was socially unacceptable to indulge in courtship, let alone marriage, during the mourning period.

When photography was still a novelty it was considered extremely unlucky for a couple, particularly if engaged, to be photographed together. And no couple hoping for a lifetime of happiness would dare to look into a mirror together for fear of breaking their bond. Even more disastrous for a girl was to wear a ring on her 'engagement finger' before a man had proposed to her. This would, it was said, condemn her to being an old maid.

How many sweethearts might you have before you find the one that's right for you? One old way of finding out is to pull your fingers one by one. The number of fingers whose joints 'crack' when tugged is the answer. Alternatively, at Christmas it is said that you should lift the top off your first mince pie of the season and see how many currants are stuck to the inside of the lid.

LOVE POTIONS

Countless concoctions have been used through the centuries to stimulate sexual desire. Rumour has it that the Roman poet Lucretius died by committing suicide in a wild frenzy brought about by taking a love potion.

Personal charms, which may be more effective because they are specific to a pair of lovers, consist of items such as locks of hair or nail clippings – or even blood – which are exchanged between them. But all kinds of substances have been added to love potions, often to make them taste disgusting (supposedly as a kind of shock therapy), including urine and animal skin. The use of rhino horn to improve performance and fertility, whether effective or not, has led to the near extinction of the black rhinoceros (*Diceros bicornis*).

To calm undesired passions witches were said to offer 'anaphrodisiacs', which included mouse droppings, prepared and applied as a liniment, and lizards dipped in urine.

Of all the plants added to love potions, most potent of all was the mandrake (*Mandragora officinarum*) or Circe's plant, whose root resembles a naked human body. It is even mentioned in the Bible as the stimulant that helped Leah, the wife of Jacob, bear him a fifth son. However, in his *Herball* of 1597 John Gerard was dismissive of its powers 'to cause women to be fruitful and bear children'.

FOODS OF LOVE

From oysters to rhinoceros horn, various foods have gained the reputation of being able to arouse desire. Many of these aphrodisiacs are believed to be especially potent because of their 'sexy' shapes.

Animal organs such as bulls' testes have long been supposed to stimulate the sexual appetite. The habits of the animal were also taken into account, so that fish, which reproduce with great fecundity, were thought to be effective. The flesh of the male partridge was favoured because of the bird's reputation for being able to fertilize his mate by the sound of his voice alone.

Foods such as figs, oysters, asparagus and leeks are thought to be provocative because they resemble the sex organs, and the ancient Greeks also made and ate phallic-shaped loaves in order to heighten their desire. After its introduction to Europe in the 16th century the tomato or 'love apple' acquired such a powerful reputation as an aphrodisiac that the Puritans declared it to be poisonous.

Aphrodisiacs are named for Aphrodite, the Greek goddess of love. At the festivals held in her honour in ancient Athens and Corinth, sexual intercourse with one of her priestesses was considered an act of worship.

The garden marigold got its nicknames of 'husbandman's dial' and 'summer's bride' from its purported aphrodisiac properties. It was one of the plants believed to be used by witches to make people fall in love.

Some aphrodisiacs live up to their reputation to some degree. Oysters are rich in zinc, one of the nutrients essential to sperm production. To improve libido in both men and women, today's herbalists recommend the stimulating effects of American ginseng (*Panax quinquefolius*) and ashwagandha (*Withania somnifera*), a tropical Indian plant whose name means 'the thing that has the smell of the horse' – a reference to the animal's strength and vitality.

The Rituals of Courtship

The formalities of wooing a bride are encompassed in the rituals of courtship, leading up to a formal engagement. Before the modern era of sexual freedom, occasions such as dances were then prime opportunities for both physical contact and bonding in friendship.

THE RULES OF COURTSHIP

In the days before universal suffrage, and particularly before World War I broke out, marriage was considered to be a woman's sole career. It was the task of caring parents to find suitable matches for their daughters – both socially and materially.

'Where a girl was concerned' comments Anna Sproule in *The Social Calendar* (1978), 'it was the duty of everyone – her mother, her mother's friends, her chaperon and her bill-settling father to help her achieve her ambition [of finding a husband] … She, confronted with a dashing "detrimental" or inelegible young man, might forget her overriding aim; they would remind her.'

A 'detrimental' was to be feared by parents. He was a flirt, smooth on the dance floor and almost certainly a wastrel from the wrong social class, even though he might act the part in elevated company. Less problematical was an 'indefatiguable', which a

The parents of 19th-century American girls were so anxious to see them marry well that some would even join the London Season in the hope of snaring a man with a title.

19th-century debutante described in her diary as 'either a young man who had just come out or an old beau who goes to three parties every evening and dances indiscriminately with the young, the pretty and the plain'. There was also little to fear from an 'indispensable', who would diligently fetch and carry everything for a girl, including her gloves and fan.

TOKENS OF LOVE

Whether love lasts or not, many tokens of affection, from simple flowers to expensive jewels, are exchanged between couples. Hopeful suitors of the past sometimes presented their girlfriends with more practical gifts – perhaps in anticipation of future domestic bliss.

Trinket boxes, pincushions, spoons and other wooden items such as butter prints and rolling pins were among the useful items traditionally given and received during courtship. But no girl, it is still said, should knit her boyfriend a sweater. If he accepts it, the saying goes, she will be his domestic slave in future. Conversely, if a woman accepts a gift of clothing from a man she cannot then refuse to marry him.

Taking their cues from mythology, courting lads would bring gifts of

Because of its associations with luck (see p 102), salt was often included as part of a courting gift, for instance to fill a wooden box or a glass rolling pin.

the aromatic plant called southernwood or lad's love (scientifically named *Artemisia abrotanum* for Artemis, the Greek goddess with special responsibility for unmarried girls). Whether or not a girl accepted the proffered sprig was critical. A young man would also show off his skills by plaiting ears of corn into elaborate tokens. A girl who accepted and wore one was destined to be both his wife and the mother of his children.

WORDS OF LOVE

Love is sweet, so it is no accident that lovers call each other 'sweetheart' and 'honey'. In modern times, endearments such as 'Pooh', 'sausage' and 'cuddles' have also become popular, as the annual screeds of newspaper Valentine messages testify.

There is another tale surrounding the word 'sweetheart'. It is associated with Lady Devorgilla of Galloway, widow of John Balliol, a 13th-century landowner of Barnard Castle, and founder of Balliol College, Oxford. For years after her husband's death she carried a silver and ivory casket containing his embalmed heart. When she died in 1290 the casket was buried beside her alongside the high altar of the Cistercian abbey she had founded in his memory in Dumfries, Scotland, which became known as Sweetheart Abbey.

When tossing a coin, 'duke or darling?' is another expression for 'heads or tails?' It comes from the scandalous affair between Frederick Duke of York (1763–1827), who commanded the British army, and Mrs Mary Anne Clarke, who made a fortune in bribes in exchange for army commissions.

Honey and the honeysuckle flower are linked through courtship customs. Giving honeysuckle to a girl would help a shy suitor break the ice, though parents discouraged her from bringing the flower indoors as it was reputed to cause erotic dreams.

OLD MAID, OLD MAID

The spinster or old maid, who devoted her life to a career as a governess or schoolmistress, or to the unpaid job of looking after her family and running the home, was once regarded with pity. Even if love came her way she might turn down marriage in favour of duty.

The original spinsters were, in Saxon times, the women of the family who spent the winter spinning wool into yarn. In the days of Alfred the Great a woman was not considered fit to be a wife until she had spun and made a set of linen for the bed, the table and to clothe herself.

Old Maid is the name of a popular family card game. One card is removed from the pack and players have to make pairs, taking cards from each other. The person left with the last, unpaired card is the 'old maid, old maid'.

'Old maid' is an unflattering term, implying a prim nature and a woman terrified of love. However, the young woman's magazine *Atlanta* of 1891 asked: 'Have you found a companion, the one whose partner in joy or sorrow you wish to be?' If the answer was 'no' it counselled waiting, adding: 'The world's reproach of "old maid" becomes then the noble woman's crown.'

St Catherine, whose feast day falls on 25 November, is the patron saint of spinsters. Girls would go to her chapel at Abbotsbury in Dorset and give up this pleading prayer to lift the curse of their unwedded state: 'A husband, St Catherine; A handsome one, St Catherine; A rich one, St Catherine; A nice one, St Catherine; and soon, St Catherine!'

COME UP AND SEE ME SOMETIME

What exactly are the magic words that will make someone fall in love with you? Believe it or not, a panel of Japanese experts has come up with a chat-up line which, supposedly, contains all the right triggers for mutual attraction.

Just how do you start that crucial conversation? For years, 'Do you come here often?' was the cliché question, along with the more suggestive 'Would you like to see my etchings?' Nowadays the effective 'word triggers' are no more subtle, but it doesn't take a psychologist to tell you that a girl likes to hear something like, 'You look great, can I buy you a drink?'

'This time next year, let's be laughing together' is the English translation of the sure-fire Japanese chat-up line devised as a result of psychological and sociological research. Key to its success, say the experts, are the word 'together', which implies commitment, and the phrase 'this time next year', meaning that this is not a flash in the pan. And laughter is a known ingredient of a successful relationship.

'Come up and see me sometime' is the catch-phrase associated with the American vamp Mae West, though the correct quotation, from the 1933 film *She Done Him Wrong*, is: 'Why don't you come up sometime, and see me? I'm home every evening.' In her long stage and film career Mae West had many other memorable lines, including, 'You ought to get out of those wet clothes and into a dry Martini,' and 'Is that a gun in your pocket, or are you just glad to see me?'

BLIND DATE

Beginning as a light-hearted way of 'setting up' meetings between people who don't know each other, blind dating has become big business for newspapers through their 'lonely hearts' columns, and for dating agencies.

The age of innocence is gone, certainly in dating. One 2004 study of blind dates in the UK discovered that one in ten of all those going on blind dates set up through agencies or advertisements is an already-married love cheat, and over a third tell lies – mostly about their age.

The expression 'blind date' originated in the eponymous TV game show begun in the US in the 1940s and famous for being hosted from 1949–52 by America's first female in the role, Arlene Francis. It was not until 1985 that the show appeared in

Britain, fronted by Cilla Black. It was Cilla herself who had seen it in the US and suggested the idea.

Not quite blind dates were the partnerships engineered throughout history and in societies worldwide by matchmakers. As well as taking into account such important aspects as the wealth and social status of the parents, Chinese matchmakers would take special note of the birth signs of the couple and also use astrological predictions to set a wedding day.

THE JEWISH MATCHMAKER IS KNOWN AS A *SHADKHAN*.
THE MATCHMAKER WAS FAMOUSLY APOSTROPHIZED IN
SONG BY BARBRA STREISAND IN THE 1971 FILM VERSION
OF *FIDDLER ON THE ROOF*.

GOING STEADY

Between falling in love and getting engaged comes the period of going steady. In country districts, 'bed fellowship' or 'bundling' was not only a customary part of 'getting to know you', but was frequently used to prove a girl's fertility.

In some parts of Britain and northern Europe, and in the eastern US states, courting couples customarily spent nights together in the home of either set of parents. This had many practical advantages, not least that girls and boys were spared long walks home in the dark and that bed

Asked about the etiquette for unmarried couples staying overnight, Miss Manners replied, 'The Victorian solution, employed with great success at English house parties, was to put illicit couples in separate rooms but to ignore nocturnal traffic in the hallway.'

was the only warm place for courtship. Though premarital sex undoubtedly took place, girls would tie up their petticoats or nightdresses to provide at least some deterrent. However, as one American publication of 1785 truthfuly remarked, '… bundler's clothes are no defence,/Unruly horses push the fence …'

Bundling largely ended with the improvement of housing in the 19th century, but long courtships – often while saving up for a wedding – remained customary, as did, however, the quick or 'shotgun' wedding necessitated by pregnancy. In Britain the 'front room' or parlour (used by the family only on Sundays and special occasions) was often occupied by a courting couple on weekday evenings. The advent of the cinema made the back seat at the movies another warm dark place for physical exploration.

WILL YOU …?

The marriage proposal on bended knee is still many a girl's dream, even though a loving couple may live together for several years before taking the final leap into marriage. Long gone are the days when a father's approval was obligatory before a suitor popped the question.

The expression 'to pop the question' derives from a purportedly unexpected request, though a woman will very often subtly invite a proposal from the man she desires.

Times have not changed that much. Writing to the editress of *Home Chat* magazine in 1896, a self-confessed 'poor male thing' asks for help. 'I am in love with a very charming girl,' he writes, 'but am very nervous and I do not know how to propose. Do give me some advice on the subject. Do you think that many words, or few, are best on such an occasion?'

The answer was unequivocal. 'I should certainly advise you to propose to the woman you love in as few words as possible. Girls do not like to be wooed rhetorically; they want to be told that a man loves them, and they like the telling to be done with a sincerity which goes straight to the mark … Take courage; tell the girl that you love her, and want to marry her; she will not be offended – why should she, when your declaration is the highest compliment you can pay her?'

THE PROPOSAL

Any man making a proposal needs to reassure a girl of his prospects, and of the advantages of marriage, as in this old nursery rhyme:

Sukey, you shall be my wife
And I will tell you why:
I have got a little pig,
And you have got a sty;
I have got a dun cow
And you can make good cheese;
Sukey will you marry me?
Say Yes, if you please.

ENGAGED IN LOVE

A formal engagement, usually marked by the giving of a ring, is a couple's 'declaration of intent'. Until 1970 in Britain it was possible to sue for breach of promise if an engagement was broken.

In Roman times, the giving of an engagement ring sealed a bargain between families. By the Elizabethan age the tripartite 'gimmal' ring was popular. It could be broken into three parts – one each for the man, the woman and the witness – which were reunited during the wedding ceremony. Such rings, and later, single ones, were usually made of silver or gold without gems.

Before diamonds – still 'a girl's best friend' and the most popular choice of gem for an engagement ring – were mined in quantity in South Africa in the 19th century, rings would be made of silver or gold, often fashioned into a lover's knot. In the 18th and 19th centuries rings were often decorated with a whole range of stones arranged in order of their initial letters to spell out a romantic message. For instance: diamond, emerald, amethyst, ruby, epidote, sapphire, turquoise were the 'code' for 'dearest'. In France similar combinations included gems spelling '*amité*' and '*souvenir*'.

The Home Counsellor of 1950 included a long list of circumstances in which an engagement could legally be broken. These included finding 'that the other party is of bad character' or that a 'girl has been unchaste either before or after the engagement'. 'It is no excuse,' the piece concluded, 'to prove that you are already engaged to someone else.'

Given in Marriage

Marriage, though not as popular today as it once was, makes love a formal union. The many good luck superstitions of weddings are still played out in the hope that in marriage love will last and flourish.

TYING THE KNOT

This expression originates in the symbolism of joining two threads together, which in ancient times had magical associations. Bride and groom also 'get hitched' – a hitch being another word for knot although, as some couples may attest, it can also mean a noose.

The significance of the knot stems from the cord that it ties, with which objects or people can be bound together. Its protective magic circle, if broken, is believed to release the forces of evil. So strong is the symbolism of the knot that in ancient marriage ceremonies actual knots were tied to strengthen the bond between husband and wife and ensure long-lasting love and fidelity. These love knots were tied using a double length of ribbon, with two bows and four ends. Today, wedding rings are often made of bands of gold intertwined into knot patterns.

TO FIND OUT WHETHER HIS LOVE WAS TRUE, A MAN COULD PUT TWO BLADES OF GRASS INSIDE HIS SHIRT, AND THINK OF HIS SWEETHEART CONSTANTLY. TRUE LOVE WOULD MAGICALLY JOIN THE BLADES TOGETHER.

Even before she was married, a girl could use the magic of the knot. One time-honoured practice to conjure a lover was to sit tying knots in a piece of string or wool while chanting:

This knot I knit,
This knot I tie,
To see my lover as he goes by,
In his apparel and array,
As he walks in every day.

MAGICAL KNOTS
The symbolic power of knots has many uses:

- Wearing a piece of knotted cord will prevent a woman becoming pregnant.
- A knot tied in a man's points (the cords linking his doublet and hose) would weaken his potency on the wedding night.
- Untying a knot will ease the pain of childbirth.
- A string knotted in nine places and tied around the neck will cure a nosebleed.
- To make a wart disappear, tie a knot in a piece of string and bury it. The wart will follow the knot into the ground.
- Dreaming of tying or untying a knot means that all your difficulties will soon disappear.
- Untie all knots in the house after a person has died to allow their soul to be released.

RUN AWAY WITH ME

The strength of the love bond – often combined with family strife – induces many couples to elope. But if one of the couple is under the legal age of consent, what is the alternative?

If the family disapproves of a couple's love, or the law is not on your side, then there may be no alternative to running away. But it is less easy to evade the law today than it was after 1753 when runaways from England, evading the new law banning 'irregular marriages' (marriages conducted without legal preliminaries, also called Fleet marriages) could marry in the forge – with the service conducted by the blacksmith – or in one of the inns in the village of Gretna Green, just over the Scottish border.

Fleet marriages were conducted in London's Fleet prison, which was considered to be outside the jurisdiction of the Church – in the 1740s they are said to have accounted for half the weddings in London.

Twenty-one was once the legal age for consent to marriage, but now 18 is the norm in most places. In the UK, and in many US states, marriage at 16 is legal but only with parental consent, although in Michigan and Minnesota a bride can be younger. Elopement today is not as easy as it was in the 1830s, when 28-year-old John Charles Fremont, explorer of the Oregon Trail, eloped with the senator's daughter Jessie Benton. She was 17. Her mother was devastated – not because of her age but because she had high hopes of her daughter marrying the President!

THE TROUSSEAU

Once, every bride-to-be would take months or even years to assemble her trousseau of linens, clothes and household items. Of the collection, which was a much scaled-down form of dowry, particular attention was paid to underwear.

Before their weddings brides would store their trousseaus in marriage chests, often inlaid with carved or decorated panels bearing good luck symbols such as doves for happiness and pomegranates for fertility. These were later replaced by simpler

---

WHAT IT COST

Trousseau items for an American bride 'of moderate circumstances' of the 1890s, with suggested costs, included:

One negligée	$12
One bath robe	$5
Two fancy silk waists [bodices]	$20
Two dressing sacques [loose-fitting dresses] one silk and one flannel	$10
Eight sets of underwear, including one bridal set	$120
Four pairs of silk stockings	$8
Six pairs of cotton stockings	$4

---

wooden 'hope chests' or 'the bottom drawer' in which the trousseau was stored.

Advising American brides on their choice of trousseau items, *The House and Home Practical Book* of the 1890s warns that 'The glamour of romance ... often induces, in the mind of even the most practical woman, a certain aberration of judgment which leads her to choose her trousseau with reference to her taste rather than to her actual needs.' On the matter of underwear its axiom was, 'The more trimming the less value'. It favoured French garments 'cut in the newest and prettiest shapes, and daintily trimmed with lace or embroideries'.

THE WORD 'TROUSSEAU' COMES FROM THE FRENCH *TROUSSE*, MEANING 'BUNDLE'. IT WAS TRADITIONALLY PAID FOR BY THE BRIDE'S PARENTS.

A LUCKY GOWN

The making of a wedding dress is a task imbued with many rituals and superstitions. Though most wedding dresses are now bought ready made, it is still considered unlucky for the groom to see his bride in her dress before she arrives at the church.

In fashion houses where wedding dresses are handmade, many concessions are still made to superstition. First and foremost there must be no whistling, for fear of conjuring up evil spirits. Black thread – even for tacking – is taboo because of its associations with death. And, to ensure good luck, the dress is not completely finished until the actual day of the wedding.

Seamstresses often sew one of their hairs into the embroidery of a dress for luck (a hair is believed to keep witches at bay) or a coin to bring wealth. In

For good luck, a bride will be careful how she handles her veil. To avoid being deserted or unhappy she will not put it on before the day. And she should not let a friend try it on, so the superstition goes, or that friend may run off with her husband.

France it is often said that the number of years a bride will live is the same as the number of buttons on her wedding dress. A bride should have her dress made for her, not make it herself.

Rather than a veil, a bride may wear a crown of gold. This is the Eastern Orthodox tradition, also practised in Scandinavia.

THE WHITE WEDDING

White, the colour of purity, is the traditional choice for a bride, though until the 19th century both bride and groom usually married in their 'Sunday best' clothes – a practice continued today by less affluent couples.

The first 'white wedding' on record is the marriage in 1499 between Anne of Brittany and the French King Louis XII. This set the precedent for royalty and the aristocracy, but white weddings became more universal aspirations only after the French *Journal des Dames* of 1813 included a fashion plate of a white wedding dress. In 1816, the first American bride to be

CHOICE OF COLOURS

That a bride should be careful in her choice of colours is expressed in this cautionary rhyme:

Married in white, you have chosen all right,
Married in black, you will wish yourself back,
Married in red, you wish yourself dead,
Married in green, ashamed to be seen,
Married in blue, you will always be true,
Married in pearl, you will live in a whirl,
Married in yellow, ashamed of your fellow,
Married in brown, you will live out of town,
Married in pink, your fortunes will sink.

married in white, complete with a tulle veil and pearl tiara, was the
19-year-old South Carolina beauty Decima Cecilia Shubrick. Her bridegroom
was one James Hamilton Heyward.

Apart from white, colour needs to be carefully chosen. Green (except in
Norway) is thought to be a particularly unlucky colour at weddings, while blue is a lucky one, as expressed in the rhymes 'Something old, something new, something borrowed, something blue,' and 'Those dressed in blue have lovers true'.

At an orthodox Jewish wedding both bride and groom dress in white.

WITH THIS RING

The wedding band is traditionally made of gold – the metal symbolic of inner riches. The finger on which it is worn was once thought to have a direct connection with the heart.

The 'giving and receiving of a ring' as a sign of an everlasting marriage bond goes back to a custom of ancient Sumeria and relates to the literal shackling of a woman to her husband. While the ancients believed that a nerve or vein linked the third finger of the hand with the heart, in the Christian tradition the bridegroom (or the priest) placed the ring, during the marriage service, on the bride's thumb and then on each of the fingers in turn, with the words 'In the name of the Father, and of the Son and of the Holy Ghost, Amen.'

In Britain and the USA more than 80 per cent of bridegrooms now opt to wear a wedding ring, and both civil and religious services allow for a dual exchange of rings.

Softer than gold of a lower carat value, 24-carat gold is the purest that money can buy. No woman would want to wear a ring made of anything but the purest gold – and least of all one made of a copper alloy that will turn the finger green.

However, desperate couples, who have either eloped or been let down by their best man, have been known to wed using anything from a curtain ring to one from a Christmas cracker.

BLESS THE BRIDE

Whatever the form of ceremony, it is traditional for the bride to be blessed in some way – if not religiously, then through the good wishes of friends and family. Many couples remarrying after divorce have their union blessed following a civil union.

Writing in around 60 BC, the Roman poet Catullus finished his wedding poem by calling on Hymen, the god of marriage and 'only lord of lovers', to bless the married pair and bring them fertility, acknowledging that without divine aid '… the land lies bare/Of sons to guard it: only you can give it strength …' The poem ends with the words: '… you, happy pair,/God bless you. Practise your nimble youth/In the gods' undying gift.'

In a Christian marriage, the modern blessing is given following the words: 'Those whom God has joined together, let no one put asunder.' As the couple kneel the priest will say: 'God the

Father, God the Son, God the Holy Spirit, bless, preserve and keep you; the
Lord mercifully grant you the riches of his grace, that you may please him
both in body and soul, and, living together in faith and love, may receive the
blessings of eternal life.'

THE APACHE WEDDING BLESSING

This is part of a moving blessing believed to stem from native American culture:

Now you will feel no cold, for each of you will be warmth to the other.
Now there will be no loneliness, for each of you will be companion to the other.
Now you are two persons, but there is only one life before you.
May beauty surround you both in the journey ahead and through all the years,
May happiness be your companion and your days together be good
and long upon the earth.

WELL THROWN

**The tradition of throwing rice or confetti over
a newly wedded couple goes back to ancient
Greek fertility rites. The logic behind this is
simple – the fruits of the earth will bring a
fruitful marriage.**

Grain, fruit and sweetmeats were the original
confetti, scattered over a bride and groom to help
ensure that they were blessed with plenty of

*The word 'confetti'
is Italian and means
'bonbons' – in Italy it
is still the custom to
throw sweets over the
bridal pair. The word
'confectionery' has the
same root.*

healthy children. In time, the missiles became lighter; as one 1896 report records: 'Bowls filled with rose-leaves and orange blossoms have at several weddings recently been handed to the bridesmaids and groomsmen … The idea is certainly a pretty one, and much kinder in its effects than the biting rice, which frequently finds its way, quite unintentionally on the part of the throwers, into the eyes of the wedded couple.'

The girl who catches the bride's bouquet as she leaves the wedding break-fast will, it's said, be the next to marry. This custom is related to a medieval romp in which stockings were thrown at the happy couple. If one thrown by a woman landed on the groom's head, this meant she would soon be wed.

CUTTING THE CAKE

The large wedding cake is a centuries-old symbol of fertility: it was once broken over the head of the bride to symbolize the end of her virginity. Until the 19th century it was known as a bride cake.

Unlike the original, simple flat cake, flavoured with spices, the modern wedding cake is usually a series of rich fruit cakes arranged in tiers, covered with both marzipan and white fondant icing and elaborately decorated with icing flowers, ribbons and lucky silver decorations such as little horseshoes. The smallest, top tier is often kept for the couple's first anniversary or the christening of their first child.

The tiers of the modern wedding cake date back to the 18th century, when an enterprising baker was inspired by the shape of the tower of St Bride's Church in London's Fleet Street.

The richness of the cake acknowledges a wedding as a time of feasting and plenty. Its ornateness reflects the medieval banqueting tradition of 'subtleties' which, far from being understatements, were sumptuous pieces such as sculpted sugar served more as entertainment than sustenance.

The first cut into the cake is made by the bride – with help from the groom. And, as a 1950s manual explains: 'To friends who were invited to the reception but who were unable to come a small slice of wedding cake should subsequently be sent.'

NO HONEYMOON IS SWEETER

The withdrawal of a couple from society immediately after their marriage was probably first called a honeymoon in the 16th century, after the honeyed wine drunk at the wedding feast, but couples did not begin to go away from home for post-wedding holidays until some 300 years later.

The 'moon' in honeymoon is thought to have various meanings. As well as meaning 'time' or 'month' it also symbolized, through its waxing and waning, the ups and downs of married life. This symbolism is also expressed in the French *lune de miel*, but in German the honeymoon is *Flitterwochen*, which translates as 'fondling weeks'.

Before they leave for their honeymoon, the bride and groom will change from their wedding clothes into 'going away' outfits. The thrifty Victorian bride was advised to choose her going away outfit with care: 'It is well to bear in mind, for future occasions, one of two alternatives – either the useful tailor-made costume, or smarter visiting gown, wherein to return wedding calls.'

For New York brides, especially those married in haste and impecunity, Buffalo, handy for Niagara Falls, was a favourite honeymoon destination. A practice immortalized in the song 'Shuffle Off to Buffalo' from the musical *42nd Street*.

Luck

Avoiding bad luck – whether it is the misfortune of losing our money, health, friends or even our lives – is something that we all hope to do.

And irrational though superstitions may be, there are few who have not at some time in their lives crossed their fingers for luck, or studiously avoided walking under a ladder or opening an umbrella indoors as a safeguard against the disasters that life can bring. Equally, to foster the chances of being blessed with good fortune, we may go through such rituals as saying 'White rabbits' on the first of the month, or carrying a talisman in a pocket.

From the earliest times, when the gods of ancient civilizations looked benignly on those who behaved according to their divine rulings, luck has had strong links with religion. 'Touching wood', for instance, harks back to the wood of Christ's cross. Other controlling forces range from agents of the Devil, such as witches, elves and goblins to, on the good side, fairy godmothers, guardian angels and the sympathetic spirits of the departed. For ill or good these have the power, many believe, to influence our fate – and we must behave appropriately to placate them.

Most of all, the longing for luck relates to the human desire to be in control, to be immune from accidents and sudden death, not just for ourselves but for those we love. Against the odds, we even wish to be able to foretell our destiny. Whether their focus is on objects or actions, on the seasons of the year or on specific situations such as the theatre or aboard ship, the superstitions involved have both a fascinating history and a role in modern life.

Days, Months and Years

For the superstitious, timing can be all, from the day of the week to the time of the year. Many of these beliefs have links with religious practices and festivals, but they also relate to long-observed phenomena such as the phases of the moon.

EVERY DAY OF THE WEEK

From routine activities such as doing the laundry and cutting your nails to life-changing events such as getting married, choosing the most auspicious day of the week is critical to good fortune and a happy future. The names of the days reflect their association with the gods.

The Romans had an eight-day week and during the French Revolution (1789–95) a 10-day week or 'decade' was introduced; it was abandoned in 1806.

This wedding rhyme is typical of the folklore associated with choosing the right day. Sunday, though now an unusual day for a wedding except in the Jewish tradition, is said to be the luckiest day of all. Otherwise, the rhyme dictates one's possible fate:

Monday for wealth,
Tuesday for health,
Wednesday best day of all,
Thursday for losses,
Friday for crosses,
And Saturday, no luck at all.

Dividing the week into seven days relates to the four phases of the moon and to the fact that seven (see p 116) was a sacred number. Relating activities to days of the week follows the Creation recounted in Genesis, when God made, on successive days, light and darkness; the heavens and the earth; trees and plants; the sun and stars; fish and birds; cattle, wild animals and 'creeping things'; and human beings 'in his own image'. On the seventh day he rested.

The day of the week on which you are born is said to influence the life that's ahead of you. Best of all is to be born on a Sunday:

Monday's child is fair of face,
Tuesday's child is full of grace,
Wednesday's child is full of woe,
Thursday's child has far to go;
Friday's child is loving and giving,
Saturday's child works hard for a living;
But the child that is born on the Sabbath-day
Is blithe and bonny, good and gay.

NEVER ON SUNDAY

Traditionally the first day of the week – and the day of rest – Sunday is, for Christians, 'the Lord's day'. It is also (incorrectly) known as the Sabbath, which, for Jews, is the last day of the week.

The Christian practice of keeping Sunday free of work goes back to the Creation story. It was once not only a sin to work on a Sunday but domestic occupations such as sewing, knitting or darning were also viewed as sure to bring bad luck. This superstition, mentioned by Charles Dickens in *The Old Curiosity Shop*, is said to relate to 'an unfortunate maid of honour in the time of Queen Elizabeth who died

The Sunday School movement was enhanced and spread through the work of Robert Raikes, a Gloucestershire newspaper publisher, who ran the first classes in 1780 primarily to teach reading and writing.

'A SABBATH PROFANED, WHATSO'ER MAY BE GAINED, IS A CERTAIN FORERUNNER OF SORROW.' A TERRIBLE FATE CAN BEFALL TRANSGRESSORS FOR, ACCORDING TO CORNISH LORE, ANYONE DANCING ON A SUNDAY IS DESTINED TO BE TURNED TO STONE. AND SETTING SAIL ON SUNDAY IS SO INAUSPICIOUS AS TO BE A SURE WAY TO BRING ABOUT A POOR CATCH OR EVEN SHIPWRECK OR DROWNING.

from pricking her finger in consequence of working on a Sunday'.

Though it may be lucky to wed on a Sunday, it's said that 'Sunday's wooing [courting] leads to ruin'. Another old belief is that a person who holds a birthday celebration on a Sunday will not live to see another birthday.

THAT MONDAY MORNING FEELING

Black Monday was the name given to Monday 19 October, 1987, when there was a dramatic fall in stock values worldwide.

The first day of the working week, named after the Anglo-Saxon Monandoeg or 'day of the moon', is one that can set the tone for the week ahead. At some times of the year, notably Easter Monday and August Bank Holiday in the UK, and Labor Day in the USA, it is also a welcome break from routine.

It is an ancient belief that anything undertaken on a Monday will be inauspicious, as in the Welsh saying that 'work begun on Monday will never be a week old'. In Ireland, however, Monday is considered the perfect day of the week to begin any job such as mowing, digging potatoes or mending a roof.

The name St Monday (or in French, St Lundi) was given to days when shoemakers, in particular, would take a day off, acting contrary to the superstition that money coming in on a Monday morning will be followed by income on every day of the week. The idea of Bank Holiday Mondays dates back only to the Victorian era. America's Labor Day holiday, on the first Monday in September, was begun by the union leader Peter J. McGuire and first celebrated in New York City on 5 September 1882. In 1884 it was moved to the first Monday in September, and in 1894 the US Congress voted it a national holiday.

GOOD FRIDAY?

For Romans and ancient Norsemen, Friday was an auspicious day associated with love and beauty, and a perfect day for a wedding, but for Christians it is for ever associated with Christ's crucifixion.

Friday is so unlucky that, it is said, a crow would not carry a straw to its nest on that day.

The Romans called Friday *dies Veneris*, the 'day of Venus', an appellation that persists in the French *vendredi*. The English name comes from Freyja or Frigg, the Norse goddess of love and marriage.

AVOIDING TROUBLE
Things it's unlucky to do on a Friday:

MOVE HOUSE .... You won't stay there long.

BEGIN A VOYAGE...It will end in disaster.

HEAR ANYTHING NEW .... It will add a wrinkle to your face.

START A NEW TASK...It will come to no good.

GO COURTING .... You'll never meet again.

BEGIN A NEW JOB .... You'll soon get sacked.

But after the establishment of Christianity Friday became the day that every bride would avoid for her wedding. The unluckiest day of all was Friday the 13th (see p 117).

Because of its proximity to Easter, Good Friday has strong associations with both life and death. The Pennsylvania Dutch believe that a child will not get whooping cough if it is put, naked, into the wheat on Good Friday and the wheat is put, in turn, into the mill. By the same tradition a rupture (hernia) will heal if the affected person puts on to the injured body part the shelled white and yolk of an egg laid on Good Friday.

Friday is the Muslim Sabbath, a day when special prayers are said. Devout Jews stop work an hour or more before sunset on Friday, the eve of the Jewish Sabbath, in preparation for attendance at the synagogue and a traditional family meal.

MOON POWER

That lives on earth are governed by the power of the moon is a belief held from ancient times to the present day. Lunar influence is said to affect everything from the health of plants and animals to the destiny of the soul.

The moon's 'disappearance' for three days in every 28 is known as the dark of the moon.

Ever since people first saw the changing phases of the moon, and the near-human features of 'the Man in the Moon' created by sunlight shining on its mountains, they have revered and worshipped our largest satellite. Its 28-day cycle was linked to the female menstrual cycle and the ancient Egyptians worshipped the moon as the mother of the universe. To Buddhists the full moon is a symbol of perfection.

MOON BELIEFS

- If a man dreams of seeing his own image in the moon he will be the father of a son.
- The Man in the Moon is burdened with a bundle of sticks on his back because he gathered sticks on a Sunday.
- If you point at the moon you will not go to heaven.
- Point at the moon seven times and you will go blind.
- As the moon waxes so the hair and nails grow faster.
- Because the moon governs the tides it also controls life and death.

To the ancient Greeks the moon was the location of the Elysian Fields, home of the blessed dead. In Romany lore, the Saviour carries departed souls to the moon for safekeeping.

As the moon waxes or increases in size, the flesh of livestock is said to become plump and tender. By farming tradition no animal, especially a pig, would be killed during a waning moon for fear that it would be tough and stringy. Similarly, seed sown while the moon is waxing is believed to grow better, though the same is not true of the harvest, for as the Roman naturalist Pliny declared: 'All vegetable productions are cut, gathered and housed to more advantage while the moon is on the wane …'

MOONLIGHT MADNESS

The light of the moon has associations with madness and other ghastly omens. It is believed to be especially danger-ous to sleep with moonlight shining in your face – this can turn you both blind and mad.

When the moon is full and bright it is hard to believe that it has no inherent source of illumination. To be 'moonstruck' is to have your mind adversely affected by the moon, and it is no accident that 'lunacy' and 'lunar' have the same etymological root. To counteract the effect of a moon that shines into their bedroom, children have long chanted the rhyme: 'I see the moon, the moon sees me, God bless the priest that christened me ...' Another traditional way of countering the effects of moonlight is to bow or curtsey to the moon, saying 'It's a fine moon, God bless her.'

A new moon is altogether luckier, especially if you see it for the first time over your right shoulder, and in the open air – but not through a window or reflected in a mirror. It is also said that if you wish for your greatest desire on seeing the new moon then your wish will be granted. And a girl who kisses a man under the new moon will receive a gift.

As protection against losing all your money, be sure to have plenty in your pocket at the new moon.

SILVER IS THE 'MOON METAL' AND IN SCANDINAVIA WOMEN WOULD WEAR SILVER AMULETS TO PROTECT THEM FROM DANGER.

FIRST OF THE MONTH

In Roman times it was the duty of the chief priest to proclaim (in Latin, *calare*, from which we get our word 'calendar') the start of the new month. Many 'firsts' throughout the year have particular significance for love and luck, and as saints' days.

'Pinch, punch, first of the month ... and no returns' is the playground rhyme (complete with appropriate actions) that heralds the first of the month, though the spell lasts only until noon. To bring good luck you should also say 'Hares' or 'Black rabbits' three times before you go to sleep on the last day of the month and 'Rabbits' or 'White rabbits' three times on waking.

Or just make your first words on the first of every month 'White rabbits'. On any other day of the month, however, many people will refer instead to 'those furry things' to avoid bad luck.

April Fool's Day, 1 April, is a day for practical jokes, from filling the sugar bowl with salt to glueing pennies to the floor. The custom, known as *poisson d'avril* in France and 'hunting the gowk' (a gowk is a cuckoo or a fool) in Scotland, is thought to have connections with deceiving any evil spirits that may interfere with the all-important season of seed-sowing.

In the Roman calendar, the other important days, apart from the first of the month (the Calends) were the Nones and the Ides, which fell according to this rhyme:

In March [fated day of Julius Caesar],
   July, October, May,
The Ides are on the 15th day,
The Nones the 7th, and all besides
Have two days less for Nones and Ides.

FIRST AND FOREMOST
Other important monthly firsts:

* 1 JANUARY – New Year's Day, rung in for luck (see p 140).

* 1 MARCH – St David's Day, when the Welsh emblems of daffodils and leeks are worn and eisteddfods (bardic music festivals) held.

* 1 MAY – May Day, a day of ancient fertility festivals and in modern times a day commemorating the power and rights of workers.

* 1 AUGUST – Lammas, the Saxon feast of bread honouring the harvest.

* 1 SEPTEMBER – Feast of the Hermit, when bonfires are lit atop Hermit's Peak, New Mexico, in memory of the holy man Juan Maria Agnosti.

* 1 NOVEMBER – All Saints Day, when prayers are said for the dead. In New Orleans tombstones are decorated with flowers.

At Home

A safe home, lived in by healthy, happy people, is something that every family desires. This wish and need are borne out in many superstitions about the positioning and protection of a house and everything in it, including the food on the table.

HOME SWEET HOME

Choosing a new home and taking up residence is a critical matter, for an unlucky or 'impure' house will bode ill for its occupants. Your first actions when you move into a new home may set the tone for what to expect in the years ahead.

If you want to stay lucky, say the superstitious, a house on the corner of the street is to be avoided at all costs, a belief that dates back to the ancient custom of burying a condemned criminal alive beneath

To propitiate the household spirits it has been customary since ancient times to embed the skull of a human or an animal (preferably a horse) in the walls of a house.

NEW LUCK

More ways to bring good luck and prosperity to a new home:

* Take in a box of coal, a piece of bread and a plate of salt before moving in any furniture. Carry a Bible with you.
* Scatter salt in every room.
* Place a talisman on or beside the front door – in both Africa and Mexico grotesque faces, either carved or moulded in terracotta, are common.
* Never go in at the front door and walk straight out again at the back, or good luck will depart the house as you go.

a cornerstone. And to test the lucky nature of a prospective new home in advance you should always send a cat in first – if the creature stays then the house will welcome you, too. Choose your moving day with care. Moving on a Friday (see p 93) is full of bad omens.

THE KEY TO FORTUNE

The key to your home may be the key to fortune, though the home's keyhole may be a breach in its defences. And once you're installed you need to be careful with the key, as well as with the windows and stairs.

To close the chink in your home's armour, keep the key in the lock. This was once thought to be most important when there was a new baby in the home, as it would prevent fairies from stealing the infant from its bed and keep away the demons that cause nightmares.

Windows or 'wind eyes' are also holes through which evil can enter. A traditional way to prevent this is to hang up a multicoloured glass sphere or 'witch ball' for protection – it not only distracts the evil eyes of witches but absorbs the first, deadly impact of their venom. A window can also be protected with branches of propitious trees such as rowan or holly.

HOME HARMONY

In the Chinese tradition, the ancient art of geomancy or feng shui determines the most propitious position of a home and the placement of items within it in relation to the invisible lines of energy that traverse the landscape. The aim is to ward off evil influences and encourage benevolent, life-giving energy.

In Hong Kong, feng shui experts are routinely consulted during building projects. British architect Sir Norman Foster retained Koo Pak Ling in such a role during the planning of the Hong Kong and Shanghai Bank, begun in 1979.

According to the principles of feng shui, the ideal placement for a home is with hills – or failing these, tall trees – to the north, or back, and with water to the south, or front. In this way, the favourable *chi* or 'cosmic breath' is perfectly balanced with the *so chi* or 'breath of ill fortune'. Gentle undulations, or a statue, on the left side of the house will ensure that the auspicious green dragon, who dwells there and brings prosperity, is

THE UNTIMELY DEATH OF THE ACTOR BRUCE LEE AT THE AGE OF 32 IS SAID BY THE SUPERSTITIOUS TO RELATE DIRECTLY TO THE SMASHING OF HIS EIGHT-SIDED MIRROR, PUT UP OUTSIDE HIS HOME TO DEFUSE THE BAD FENG SHUI OF THE VALLEY OF KOWLOON IN WHICH IT WAS SITUATED.

dominant, rather than the unlucky white tiger on the right. An open space at the front of the house allows the beneficial *chi* to accumulate there.

Inside the home, the auspicious placement of items depends on the points of the compass. Each area of a room can be positively activated by what is placed there. For instance the north-west represents helpful or supportive people and is enhanced by metal objects. The south-east is where wealth and prosperity flourish, helped by wooden objects and anything coloured green or purple. Fortune, celebrity and attention, augmented by fire and the colour red, define the southern orientation, while in the easterly aspect of a room, also devoted to harmony, wood is again the material of choice.

HOME LUCK
Feng shui tips for a lucky home:

- Avoid clutter, which causes positive energy to stagnate, and items with sharp edges, which can aim 'poison arrows' at you.
- Never place a mirror on the wall facing your bed, because the spirit leaves the body at night and may be disturbed by seeing its own reflection.
- Do not sleep with your feet facing the door, since this is how corpses are laid out to give them easy access to heaven.
- Place an eight-sided mirror on the front of your home to deflect negative energy.
- Prevent energy from flowing directly, and too quickly, from the front to the back door of the house by erecting screens.

EDIBLE OMENS

Of all the foods in the house, bread, 'the staff of life', is the one most richly associated with ancient beliefs and omens. While for pagan peoples it was the embodiment of the corn spirit, for Christians it is an essential element of the sacrament of the Eucharist.

Such was the value of bread to our forebears that throwing it away or burning it was considered sacrilegious and would not only make the Virgin

Mary cry but would ensure that those who committed this act would go hungry. Throwing crumbs in the fire was called 'feeding the Devil'. Making a cross in the bread dough before it is put in a warm place to rise is believed to protect this most precious food from being stolen or contaminated by the Devil or by witches.

When the bread comes out of the oven, it must be treated with care and never pricked with a knife or allowed to stand upside down on the table, even by accident. If, when broken open, a loaf is discovered to have a long hole or 'coffin' inside, this is an omen of death. And while it is unlucky to take the last slice of bread and butter from the plate, especially if you are a woman in search of a husband, to take the last slice when offered is, by long tradition, worth either 'a handsome husband or £10,000 a year'.

Cut with care: slicing a loaf from the bottom to the top means you will not rise in the world. Cut it unevenly and riches and success will elude you for ever.

A SPRINKLE OF SALT

Known as a food preserver since ancient times, salt is the symbol of purity and incorruptibility. The respect that salt is afforded reflects both its protective force and undoubted value. Because of its purity, salt has long been used in rituals of birth and death.

Putting a pinch of salt – and one of sugar – as a first gift to newborn babies' mouths is an old way of protecting them from evil and ensuring prosperity. At the end of life, salt is often put inside a coffin or set on a pewter plate beside the body: this is said to protect the newly departed from evil spirits, especially when their soul is hovering between heaven and hell.

To eat another man's salt – that is, to share it with your host – is to create an unbreakable bond between you. Salt protects a home when new (see p 98), and at every New Year, while keeping salt in your pocket is still a customary way of guarding against the forces of evil. To 'unlock' a bad spell from something, an old tradition is to stir a mixture of salt and water three times, sign it with a cross and sprinkle it over the fated object.

The unlucky effect of spilling salt is said to go back to Leonardo da Vinci's portrayal of Judas spilling salt in *The Last Supper*. To neutralize it, a pinch should be thrown with the right hand over the left shoulder. An old Yorkshire saying is that you must shed a tear for every grain of salt you spill.

SALTY SAYINGS

The value of salt is revealed in many phrases and sayings:

SALT OF THE EARTH .... Perfection. Said of a worthy and honest person.

SALT AWAY .... To preserve for the future.

BREAD AND SALT .... To take an oath. Salt was sometimes used instead of the Bible for this purpose.

WORTH ONE'S SALT .... Deserving of pay. The word 'salary' derives from the Latin *salarium* – a soldier's pay or 'salt money', which was sometimes paid in salt itself.

SALT OF YOUTH .... The vigour and passion of the young.

OLD SALT .... An experienced sailor, well versed in the ways of the sea.

Luck on the Land

Ensuring the future of the harvest, the health of animals and safety in their daily lives are the prime considerations of all who work on the land and have been so for centuries as age-old rituals confirm.

FARMING FORTUNE

The judicious farmer takes care to propitiate the spirit of the harvest and to tend his crops and animals in a way that will make for all-round abundance. Such traditions doubtless began when the success of the harvest was literally a matter of life or death.

On Plough Monday, the first Monday after Twelfth Night and the first workday of the year, the custom was for men to dress up in gaudy costumes decorated with ribbons and flowers, to take a 'white plough' from door to door. Here they would ask for money to spend on food and wine.

A good crop begins with preparing the soil with the plough. While any farmer would want straight furrows in his fields, it is an old custom to leave one furrow – especially one near the farmstead – deliberately crooked. This was to lead the eye of the 'evil one' away from human habitation, or so that fairies who, according to one account of 1895, 'took a malicious pleasure in shooting their fatal bolts at the patient beasts of burden ...' could not aim their arrows along the furrows.

Another customary way of driving evil away from the crops is with sound. In many parts of the world, the ringing of church bells is thought to be able to expel evil spirits from the fields. The sound of wassailing at Twelfth Night, so it is said, will encourage good growth, particularly of an apple crop. By ancient tradition cider was poured on the roots of the best tree in the orchard, and the tree was toasted and sung to as if it were human.

'Wassail' means 'be in [good] health'. The tuneful salutation is traditionally made over a wassail bowl filled with ale or cider, often with spices added, whose contents are then drunk.

HARVEST HOME

A good harvest brings the assurance of food to last the winter and good seed corn to plant for the following year. So the old harvest traditions give thanks for the year past and look forward to abundance to come.

To give thanks for the harvest the Greeks turned their devotions to the earth goddess Demeter, and in many places the belief that her spirit was embodied in the final sheaf of corn persisted well into the Christian era. To keep her spirit alive, the last ears of the crop were woven into corn dollies, which were kept until spring then ploughed into the earth. To help cattle to thrive over the winter the last sheaf of corn was often dressed in women's clothes and laid in the manger.

Early Christian priests would bless the crop, but after the Reformation in the 16th century the practice largely died out until it was revived in Victorian times. The American celebration of Thanksgiving began in 1621, in Plymouth Colony,

In Greek mythology, Demeter (her name means 'mother earth') had a cult centred at Eleusis, south of Athens, which became the centre of a mystery religion in which secret rites were performed (see p 223).

when the Pilgrims who had arrived in Massachusetts gave thanks that their new land had been good to them. The festival was adopted from the festival of Lammas or Loaf Mass Day, celebrated on 1 August, when farmers would bring loaves to share with the community as tokens of gratitude.

The harvest moon, which near the autumn equinox rises for several days at around sunset, illuminates the sky in almost mystical fashion. Rider Haggard evocatively described it in *A Farmer's Year* (1899): 'This evening ... I watched the rising of the harvest moon. She appeared in an absolutely cloudless sky, a huge and lambent all, pale at first, but growing brighter with each passing minute ... and when man, having gathered his last harvest, has returned to the Lord of harvests, still that light, piercing the gulf of airless space, will flow upon this hillside, and creep down yonder valley, grown black and dead, and desolate.'

BEWARE THE HAGS

The fortunate farmer will rear fat, fertile livestock, untroubled by accident and disease. But there are legends and superstitions in every land that are intended to ensure the health of all the animals, from horses to sheepdogs, on which country folk rely.

For as long as we have relied on animals for food, keeping valuable stock healthy has been paramount, and legend has it that keeping witches

Luck with domesticated animals begins with the manner in which they are acquired. If given a good offer you should always, it's said, sell an animal to someone who really wants it — otherwise it will sicken and die.

at bay is critical. To nullify the evil eye, and to prevent 'hag-riding' – the practice of witches and fairies exhausting horses and cows by galloping them over the fields at night, making them break out in a sweat and tangling their manes in knotted 'elf-locks' – many farmers still hang their stable keys on a 'hag stone' at night. This stone is a flint with a hole in it that is naturally formed (but it is believed to have been penetrated by fairies) and represents the all-seeing eye.

Other deterrents to hag-riders were silver and lucky iron implements, especially those shaped in the form of a cross, as this old rhyme explains:

Hang up Hooks and Sheers to scare
Hence the Hag, that rides the Mare,
Till they be all over wet,
With the mire, and the sweat:
This observ'd, the Manes shall be
Of your horses, all knot-free.

PRECIOUS CATTLE

Cattle, which are sacred to Hindus, have long been regarded in other traditions as creatures with supernatural powers. Some farmers continue to believe that these animals can share the joys and sorrows of their owners.

That cattle may have near-human qualities is borne out by the legend that on the stroke of midnight on Christmas Eve they turn to the east and kneel in adoration of the infant Jesus, in honour of their ancestors who witnessed the event.

The ancestor of today's domestic cattle was the aurochs, a massive, fierce, horned beast. Cattle were probably first domesticated in Turkey in around 6000 BC and brought to western Europe some two millennia later.

In some places, stolen hay was always added to their Christmas Day feed to bring luck.

Cattle death – as modern epidemics of foot and mouth disease testify – is still a cause for grief and concern. The old way of stopping any disease spreading through a herd was to hang the leg of a dead animal in the chimney for protection. Winding red thread around cattle horns was also believed to keep them safe (red being a curing colour, see p 154). As soon as a cow gave birth it was also customary to rub salt on her back to prevent milk fever.

IN MANY MYTHOLOGIES THE COW IS REVERED AS THE GREAT MOTHER, PROVIDER OF MILK TO HER PEOPLE. IN EGYPT HER INCARNATION WAS HATHOR, WHOSE UDDERS PRODUCED THE MILKY WAY AND WHO DAILY GAVE BIRTH TO THE SUN. HER PROGENY, THE GOLDEN CALF, WAS THE ANIMAL WORSHIPPED BY THE ISRAELITES IN THE OLD TESTAMENT.

Luck at Sea

At sea, danger lurks night and day from the waves and the weather. This is ample reason, therefore, to be sure of optimizing your good fortune in everything from the construction of a vessel to what's taken on board. For fisher folk, 'good' behaviour while on board may also help to ensure a fruitful catch.

Until 1977, the US Navy kept alive the custom of novitiates being sent below decks to polish the imaginary 'golden rivet' set in the darkest corner of the hull.

BUILDING FOR LUCK

A lucky ship is one that will withstand the most powerful forces of the ocean and preserve the lives of the men aboard from dangers of all kinds, even those engendered by war. If it is a fishing vessel, a lucky ship will ensure plentiful and abundant catches.

In its building, a ship can be endowed with good luck, so many believe, in the way that it is constructed and decorated. The heart of a ship is the keel, the lowest longitudinal piece of timber or line of metal plates. To bring good luck the first nail inserted to keep it in place is often banged in through the hole in a horseshoe. At this stage a toast may be drunk.

Bones, shoes and gold are traditionally hidden in the ship during its construction to bring good luck, but their position must be kept secret if the charm is not to be broken.

In ship building, black walnut, though strong, was a wood traditionally rejected because it was thought to attract lightning. And even if oak was used for the keel, other woods were also inserted in some way (for instance as rivets) to bring luck by keeping witches at bay. Among them were ash, rowan and dogwood.

The day of the week on which a keel was laid was important. Days to avoid were Thursday, dedicated to Thor, the god of thunder, and Friday, the day of Frigg, the beautiful but dangerous wife of the Norse god Odin.

FORTUNATE FIGUREHEADS

The ancients looked to their deities to protect their ships against disaster and this is the origin of both ships' figureheads and their names. To this day, ships are painted with 'oculi', or symbolic eyes, to keep evil spirits at bay.

The Roman poet Ovid summed up the importance of figureheads and names when he declared: 'My guardian deity is yellow-haired Minerva – and may she be such, I pray … My ship,' he continued, 'takes name from a painted helmet [on a bust of the goddess] on the bow.' While the Phoenicians favoured horses' heads, symbols of speed, Greek figureheads were often boars, representing aggression. Dragons, lions and unicorns were later popular on the warships of many countries.

Most modern ships do not carry figureheads, but the idea of a talisman is often incorporated into ships' crests and badges.

MOST FIGUREHEADS WERE FEMALE – INCLUDING LEGENDARY FEMALE FIGURES SUCH AS MERMAIDS – BUT IN 1834 THE USS *CONSTITUTION* WAS GIVEN THE FIGUREHEAD OF PRESIDENT ANDREW JACKSON, DEPICTED WEARING A CLOAK AND HAT. IN HIS HAND HE HOLDS A SCROLL BEARING THE US CONSTITUTION.

The massive oculi on the canoes of Easter Islanders are made of mother of pearl, while the tradition in Malta is to decorate fishing boats with eyes complete with eyebrows. These 'eyes of Horus' protect against the evil eye. Without its eyes a boat is believed to be 'blind' and unable to see its way forward in safety. Later figureheads often incorporated oculi in the form of large staring eyes.

I NAME THIS SHIP …

Every ship needs a lucky name – and a naming ceremony before she sets sail. An unlucky name like *Titanic* is never repeated, but lucky ones continue through many generations of vessels.

It is deemed extremely unlucky to launch a ship before she is named, or to change her name. Delaying the launch after the naming ceremony is also said to bring bad luck.

In most parts of the world, ships are definitely feminine, though France is a notable exception. And although women's names – from the *Mary Rose* to *Empress of the Seas* and *Pocahontas* – are common, animal names are redolent of success and strength at sea, from *Lynx* and *Tiger* to *Bulldog*. A ship named *Fair Breeze* will attract good winds, and speed will come with a name like *Dolphin*. Also popular are the simple *Lady Luck* and *Fortuna Redux*, meaning 'good luck that brings you home'.

Until the 1800s a ship was launched by having wine poured over her bow from a silver goblet, which was then thrown into the water as a gift to Poseidon, god of the deep. Nowadays a bottle of champagne tied to a fancy cord and, for a large liner, a celebrity 'namer', is the more likely scenario.

The custom of breaking wine over a ship to launch her evolved from the blood baptisms practised by the Vikings. A prisoner was lashed to the ship and sacrificed – his blood served to bless the vessel.

KNOCKING AWAY THE BLOCKS ON WHICH SHE STANDS, SO FREEING A SHIP FOR LAUNCHING, WAS A DANGEROUS JOB ONCE GIVEN TO CRIMINALS. ANY DEATH OR INJURY AT THE LAUNCHING WAS THOUGHT TO JINX A SHIP FOR EVER.

A GOOD CATCH

Since men first set sail to harvest the ocean's living crop, fishermen have held to all manner of superstitions, whether to ensure good weather, keep the crew safe or bring fish to lines and nets.

Compared with hooked fishing lines, which have been in use for at least 27,000 years, fishing nets are relatively new. They were first used by the ancient Egyptians, who made them from plaited plant fibres and thongs of hair and leather. For luck – and fish a-plenty – fishermen still insert coins in the cork floats and draw their fishing lines through a fire. And they will begin work mending their nets only when the tide is flowing.

On board, fishing tradition has it that it is unlucky to count either fish or boats, and that more fish will be attracted to a line or net if the first fish caught – especially if a salmon or ling – is thrown overboard. Urinating over the ship's side before the nets are cast is another good way of luring fish, but it is said that herrings will be deterred for ever if their scales are deliberately washed from a fisherman's boots.

Women play an important, although negative, role in fishing lore. A woman walking over nets or fishing tackle means a poor catch, and in the past fishermen would abandon their trips in fear of their lives if they met a woman in a white apron before they put to sea.

A marriage among fisherfolk is believed to be a sure way of provoking stormy weather – but so, it's said, is having a prostitute on board ship.

SAFE AT SEA

Whether braving the seas for pleasure, to fish, or to defend the nation, sailors the world over are concerned for their personal welfare and the integrity of their ships. In ancient times, the ship itself was an object of worship.

Ships have long been associated with death, from the Norse death ships that took the departed back to their mother-sea to the boat which, according to Egyptian legend, carried away Osiris, the lord of death. Considering the might of the open

If death occurred at sea, the naval rite was to sew the corpse into a shroud with the last stitch made through the nose to ensure that a man was truly dead. This practice also ensured that his ghost would not haunt the ship.

ocean it is hardly surprising that sailors will do all they can to preserve their lives at sea.

Symbols of doom are therefore critical at sea. Overturned bowls and buckets are taboo because they represent capsized boats, and there is an obvious connection between a cat drowned at sea and the loss of human life. Also unlucky at sea are lost brooms, boots carried on the shoulder, untied knots and – surprisingly – the act of saving a drowning stranger. Pins are never taken on board because they are the embodiment of spiteful witches.

WHEN A SHIP CROSSES THE LINE – THAT IS, THE EQUATOR – IT IS TRADITIONAL TO PAY TRIBUTE TO THE GOD NEPTUNE, THOUGH NO LONGER WITH A HUMAN SACRIFICE. IN ANCIENT TIMES THE PHOENICIANS CONDUCTED RITUALS AT THE PILLARS OF HERCULES, ON THEIR ENTRY INTO THE ATLANTIC FROM THE MEDITERRANEAN.

CREATURES OF THE DEEP

Seafarers have long feared attack from sea serpents and other creatures of the deep, including the legendary mermaids whose wiles entrap unwary or ungrateful fishermen. Sailors are also wary of birds – particularly the albatross, gull and storm petrel.

The mermaid, with the upper torso of a woman and the tail of a fish, seduces sailors, it is said, with her long hair and beautiful singing. But to stay benign she must be appeased, according to legend, with gifts such as gold and silver. However, the 'real' mermaids of the sea are most probably seals, dugongs and manatees which, according to folklore, have the habit of seeking out human company.

Sailors treat all gulls with respect in case one of them is the reincarnation of a drowned shipmate. An albatross that follows a ship brings good fortune and, as Samuel Taylor Coleridge's poem 'The Ancient Mariner' famously relates, luck will desert anyone who harms or kills this bird.

The sea monster, capable of wrecking a boat or drowning its crew, takes on many guises. The Roman naturalist Pliny described an octopus-like creature. 'No animal,' he said, 'is more savage in causing the death of a man in the water; for it … drags him asunder by its multiple suction, when it attacks men that have been shipwrecked.' The sea serpent described by a New England sailor, even as late as 1802, as being '… of a colour as blue as possible … [with a] black ring round his eye', harks back to the myth of Jormungand, the Scandinavian Midgard Serpent, inhabitant of the ocean floor, which created storms when it 'heaved its scaly coils'.

Storm petrels (*Hydrobates pelagicus*) are aptly named because these birds are seen inland only when blown there in bad weather. Sailors know them as 'witches'. The birds' habit of pattering their feet against the water may be the origin of the name 'petrel', or it may be linked to St Peter who, like these birds, walked on water.

Lucky Numbers

Numbers have long associations with good luck and bad. From the auspicious unity of one to 666, the legendary 'number of the beast', numbers can, many believe, affect our fortunes. And life ends, it is said, when your number is up.

THE POWER OF NUMBERS

Whether counted on the fingers, or written in Egyptian hieroglyphs, Roman numerals or the Arabic numbers we use today, numbers have great significance in our lives. In the ancient world, they held the keys to understanding, explaining how the universe was organized and the magical forces that could change the course of human life, for good or bad.

The relationship between luck and numbers was culture-specific. In Babylonian society the numbers from one to 60 were reserved for the gods, while the ancient Chinese deemed even numbers to be male and less lucky, and odd ones female and luckier. Today, 13 is the most unlucky number, but while bad things are said to happen in threes, it is also possible to be 'third time lucky'.

Numbers have long played a significant part in astrological predictions. Traditionally astrologers believed that the seventh and ninth years, and their multiples – especially 21, 27 and other odd numbers – were particularly significant (climacteric) years in which malevolent influences held sway. Sixty-three, which is nine times seven, was the age beyond which people once aspired to live.

THE PERFECT SEVEN

The notion of the seven-year itch, identifying the time when a marriage is at its most vulnerable, is thought to come from the Roman belief that the mind and body renew themselves every seven years.

It is no accident that, in the fairy tale, Snow White went to live with seven dwarfs, then overcame the Queen's evil power and married her Prince Charming. For seven is a lucky number – the number of days in the week, ages of man and gifts of the Holy Spirit. But break a mirror and, it is said, you will have seven years' bad luck.

Seven, the sum of four and three – both lucky numbers – is the number of the sacred planets recognized by the ancient Egyptians and

Babylonians, each with its own heaven. According to the alchemists, there were seven metals, each corresponding to one of these planets, the best of all being gold. Seven has also been associated with good fortune ever since Noah obeyed God's word and led seven pairs of clean animals and seven pairs of birds of the air (as well as two each of the unclean animals) into the ark. After the flood, the rainbow, the eventual signal of God's treaty with humankind, was made to consist of seven colours.

The pinnacle of ecstasy or good fortune is said to take us to seventh heaven, which is the height of Muslim aspiration after death. The first of these heavens, the abode of Adam and Eve, is 'pure silver; here the stars, each with an angel warder, are hung out like lamps on golden chains.' The seventh heaven is 'formed of divine light, beyond the power of the tongue to describe'. Each inhabitant has '70,000 tongues and each tongue speaks 70,000 languages, all for ever employed in chanting the praises of the Most High'.

Babylonian astronomers periodically added a short thirteenth month to their lunar calendar to keep it in step with solar time, but it was considered so unlucky that for its duration all activities ground to a halt.

UNLUCKY THIRTEEN

When, on the eve of Good Friday, Jesus sat down to the Last Supper there were 13 people at the table. The 13th, Judas Iscariot, was soon to betray Christ, an act that culminated in his crucifixion. So 13, and especially Friday the 13th, is believed to have gained its association with bad luck.

From this belief stems the superstition that 13 people should never sit at table together or one of the party will die within the year, most probably the person who is first to rise from their chair. Similarly, one member of a ship's crew of 13 is believed to be destined for a fatal accident, 13 being known as 'the Devil's lot'. Or unlucky 13 could come from the number in a witches' coven, of which the 13th is the most evil.

IRRATIONAL FEAR OF THE NUMBER 13 IS KNOWN AS TRISKAIDEKA-
PHOBIA. IN THE STREETS OF MANY TOWNS, HOUSES ARE NUMBERED 12A
RATHER THAN 13; THE SAME APPLIES TO THE NUMBERING OF HOTEL
ROOMS AND THE FLOORS IN SOME SKYSCRAPERS.

SAFETY IN NUMBERS?

Whether odd numbers are more lucky than even ones depends on both culture and custom, but there are many variations. The objects and actions associated with certain numbers are significant too, whether you're counting magpies or a run of accidents.

Just as we give three cheers for a fortunate event and believe that we can be third time lucky, so it's commonly held that accidents happen in runs of three, then stop – for a while, at least. That three, the number of the Holy Trinity, is also an odd number may be significant, too. In both Eastern and Western lore, odd numbers (with the notable exception of 13) are considered lucky: the Roman poet Virgil noted in around 40 BC that 'odd numbers please the gods'.

To prevent toothache, Pliny advocated washing the mouth out with cold water every morning 'an odd number of times'.

Consistency, however, there is not. Many deem it unlucky to have an odd number of people seated around the table or at a funeral party. In the latter case it is said that the deceased will call for another soul to even up the numbers. Numbers are also a sensitive issue when it comes to magpies – seeing a lone bird is bad, but two or more are lucky, as in the rhyme 'One for sorrow, two for joy, three for a girl, four for a boy ...' The number of times you sneeze may be significant. Sneeze once and someone is speaking well of you, sneeze twice and the reverse is true. Or test your luck according to the verse:

Once a wish,
Twice a kiss,
Three times a letter,
Four times something better.

Luckiest of all is for two people to sneeze simultaneously.

Taking Action for Luck

Many actions are believed to influence our luck. These may involve specific objects or, as in meeting certain animals, demand that something is done to neutralize the ill effects of some accidental occurrence. Very often, the origins of such superstitions have their roots in religious beliefs.

THE UPS AND DOWNS OF UMBRELLAS

The Chinese are credited with inventing umbrellas around 1000 BC, and with the superstition that they should be opened only outdoors. The belief persists today: holding an open umbrella over your head while inside the house is still thought to be an omen of death.

For the ancient Chinese, putting up an umbrella indoors was believed to be an insult to the sun

The umbrella gets its name from the Italian ombrella *meaning 'little shadow'. The French* parapluie *literally means 'against the rain'.*

because they worshipped our warmth-giving star as a deity. Their original umbrellas were made of bamboo covered in silk, and were probably not waterproof, but by the 6th century AD they were covering umbrellas with oiled mulberry bark, which was indeed rain-resistant.

In Britain even opening an umbrella was once thought to be ungodly. Clerics of the time said it was the Lord's purpose that people should get wet if it rained. The philanthropist Jonas Hanway, who regularly used one from the 1750s, is said to have been the first Londoner to break the taboo.

A British Guards officer, when off duty in civilian dress in London, may carry a rolled umbrella, but under no circumstances should he open it. The command dates back to the Battle of Salamanca in 1812 where the Duke of Wellington was appalled to see officers sheltering under umbrellas and banned their use thereafter.

UMBRELLA LORE

Many superstitions relate to both umbrellas and sunshades:

- It is unlucky to give an umbrella as a gift.
- Tragedy will follow if you put an umbrella on the bed.
- If you drop an umbrella, do not pick it up yourself. Let someone else do so and you will avert evil fortune. On no account should you thank them ...
- ... But the person who picks up another's dropped umbrella will themselves attract good fortune.

FINGERS CROSSED

For the superstitious, crossing the fingers, specifically the index and second fingers of the right hand, is the way to avert bad luck or to bring about a lucky event. Some people also cross their legs for good luck but oldest of all is thumb holding.

The act of finger crossing is believed to relate to the sign of the Cross, which is made by Christians to revere, recognize and remember Christ's crucifixion, though this is based on no hard evidence. There are specific circumstances in which finger crossing is thought to be particularly protective – for instance after walking under a ladder or seeing a single magpie. Crossing the fingers while telling a lie is a way of receiving protection against the consequences of this ill deed.

CROSSING THE LEGS FOR LUCK MAY BE AN EVEN OLDER PRACTICE THAN CROSSING THE FINGERS, AND WAS PARTICULARLY COMMON AMONG GAMBLERS. IT WAS CERTAINLY KNOWN BY THE 17TH CENTURY.

Holding the thumb within the fingers of the same hand to keep away ghosts was recorded by Ovid in AD 17, and in his *View of Northumberland* of 1778 W. Hutchinson records that, 'Children, to avoid approaching danger, are taught to double the thumb within the hand. This was much practised while the terrors of witchcraft remained.' It was also, he says, 'the custom to fold the thumbs of dead persons within the hand to prevent the power of evil spirits over the deceased'.

THE POWER OF TOUCH

We touch or knock on wood to protect ourselves from tempting fate, to bring an ambitious wish to fruition, or to nullify the effects of bragging or boasting. Touching iron – an older practice – is a way of avoiding the misfortune that comes from uttering a 'forbidden' word, especially on a ship, or confronting a witch or other malign being.

For the Celts, the yew tree was a symbol of immortality; they used it to make shields which, as well as acting as armour in battle, were thought to have magical powers that protected them from death.

The habit of touching wood may have originated from an ancient belief in tree spirits, but probably coincided with the 10th-century practice of venerating holy relics and touching them to gain protection from their sanctity. But, according to tradition, only certain woods will do. Because magic and religious rituals favoured the use of such trees as oak, yew, hazel, ash and hawthorn, these were the ones that would confer the greatest protection. Hornbeam, the exclusive material of sorcerers' wands, was also especially favoured.

Touching iron was common among the fishermen of Scotland, as reported in *Scottish Customs* of 1885: 'If, when at sea … any one was heard to take the name of God in vain, the first to hear … immediately called out "cauld iron", when each of the boat's crew would instantly grasp fast the first piece of iron which came within reach.' In the playground, touching iron in a game of tag is a traditional way of being 'safe' from capture.

On board ship, saying the word 'pig' was, and is, particularly unlucky, and would have to be counteracted by touching iron.

HANG UP A HORSESHOE FOR LUCK

But be sure it is the right way up. Unless the open end or heel is placed uppermost, the good luck will fall out. It is also lucky to find a cast horseshoe, pick it up and keep it.

As the *Discoverie of Witchcraft* of 1584 relates (translated into modern spelling), the 'rule observed in many country houses', in order 'to prevent and cure all mischieves wrought by these charms and witchcrafts', was that it was advisable to 'nail a horse shoe at the inside of the outmost threshold of your house, and so you shall be sure no witch shall have the power to enter.' Advice from around the same period is specific about the orientation of the shoe and that three nails should be used.

Horseshoes probably originated in Eurasia around the 2nd century BC. In Europe, Roman horseshoes have been discovered dating from the late third century AD. Shoes meant that horses could travel farther and last longer in battle.

Another old explanation of the horseshoe's ability to waylay evil is that, because the Devil always moves in a circle, he is stopped in his tracks by the gap in the horseshoe and is

FOR NEED OF A NAIL

That fortune may be linked to horseshoe nails is borne out in this well-known children's rhyme:

For want of a nail the shoe was lost
For want of a shoe the horse was lost
For want of a horse the rider was lost

For want of a rider the battle was lost
For want of a battle the kingdom was lost
And all for the want of a horseshoe nail.

'obliged to take a retrograde course'. Adding to the horseshoe's luckiness is the fact that it is made of iron, and therefore can be touched for luck.

AS WELL AS PICKING UP A HORSESHOE, IT IS ALSO LUCKY TO PICK UP A HORSESHOE NAIL, AND – FOR EVEN GREATER GOOD FORTUNE – TO USE IT TO HANG UP THE HORSESHOE. EVERY ORIGINAL NAIL USED IN THE HANGING IS SAID TO BRING A WHOLE YEAR OF LUCK.

WELL MET?

The animals that cross your path may, according to superstition, seriously affect the way your day – or even your life – turns out. For as one John of Salisbury recorded as long ago as 1159, 'You may ascertain the outcome of your journeys from beasts …'

That hares are thought mad (like the Mad Hatter in Alice's Adventures in Wonderland) relates to their habit, in spring, of rearing up on their hind legs and 'boxing'. The pair are either two competitive males or an ardent male and a reluctant female beating off his advances.

Hares have particular resonances for travellers because they are believed to be the incarnations of witches and, in this disguise, would rob cows of their milk. However, an old way of negating the bad luck of meeting a hare is to spit over your left shoulder and say: 'Hare before,/Trouble behind:/ Change ye, Cross, and free me'. Another animal whose form witches take is the weasel, which is believed to presage the death of humans and beasts whose paths it crosses.

Good luck will be yours, it's said, if you meet a piebald horse. And wishing while curtseying to the creature nine times backwards will make the wish come true. Your wish will also come true if you cross your fingers when you meet a piebald horse and keep them crossed until you see a dog. When you meet an all-white horse, however, you should also spit and wish for luck.

ANIMAL CHARMS

Be careful when you meet these animals — they may bring you good luck or bad, though sailors and fishermen believe that all four-legged creatures are ill omens.

SNAKE .... Watch out for false friends if it crosses your path.

PIG .... A disappointment is due, unless a sow has a litter of piglets with her, in which case your luck is in.

TOAD OR FROG .... Money is on its way to you.

DOG .... If a strange dog follows you beware of bad luck.

CAT .... In Britain, a cat crossing your path is lucky if black, unlucky if white; in most other places the reverse is true.

SHEEP.............................. Luckiest if in a flock, but it is unlucky to count them.

TRAVELLERS' LUCK

However you travel it has long been deemed unlucky to turn back once your journey has begun, though there are ways of breaking the spell. For safety 'insurance', many people carry or wear a talisman of some kind.

Some say the origin of the 'looking back' superstition goes back to the Bible story of Lot's wife who, when she did this as she left the doomed city of Sodom, was turned into a pillar of salt. More probably it originated in medieval times with the pronouncement of John of Salisbury that, 'If one is called back as he starts his journey he should not on that account, if he has set out with the blessing of the Lord, give it up.'

TO AVOID RE-ENTERING THE HOUSE FOR A FORGOTTEN ITEM THE SUPERSTITIOUS WILL CALL FOR IT FROM THE ROAD OR GARDEN GATE. ANOTHER WAY OF CHEATING THE FATES IS TO SIT INDOORS FOR A FEW MINUTES 'TO BREAK THE SPELL'.

The wild clematis (Clematis vitalba) was named 'traveller's joy' by the 16th-century herbalist John Gerard because, although it had no medicinal properties, it lifted the hearts of travellers, especially in winter when covered with the feathery white seeds that give it the alternative name of 'old man's beard'.

That St Christopher is the patron saint of travellers comes from the legend that this giant of a man once sought to serve God by carrying people across a ford in a fast river, oblivious of danger to himself.

One day a small child asked to be carried, and the giant found him heavier than any other burden. In reply to his declaration: 'Child, thou hast put me in great peril. I might bear no greater burden,' the child (who revealed himself to be Christ) replied: 'Marvel thou nothing for thou hast borne all the world upon thee and its sin likewise.' He baptized the giant, giving him the name Christopher, which means 'Christ carrier'.

Other saints also protect travellers, including St Raphael, dubbed by Milton 'the affable archangel', and St Antony of Padua, a 13th-century monk whose ship was wrecked by a storm on the coast of Sicily when he was sailing from Africa to Portugal.

Theatrical Luck

Of all professionals, actors and actresses are undoubtedly among the most superstitious. From the moment they enter the dressing room for rehearsals to the end of the run, everything has to be just right to ensure, most of all, a successful show and more roles to follow.

THESPIAN FORTUNE

Maybe it is their nature – and the nature of their profession – that makes actors and actresses among the most superstitious folk around, whether in their dressing rooms, in rehearsal or on stage.

Drama probably evolved out of the annual festivals held by the ancients to celebrate the coming of spring and the abundance of the harvest when, to assure future good fortune, deities were thanked in song and dance. In the Greek festivals to honour Dionysus, god of the vineyard, trees, plants and fruitfulness, the leader of a village procession would engage in dialogue with his company and with leaders of rival bands, and it is these dialogues that evolved into the Greek comedies. Similarly, the spring recounting of the tales of the gods were the seeds of the Greek tragedies.

Religion was also a formative influence on the theatre and its traditions. In the Middle Ages, dramas telling the life of Christ were performed in churches, and these developed into the cycles of Mystery and Miracle plays in which,

---

GOOD LUCK CHARMS
Lucky talismans have a particular power for actors and actresses, including:

- DOLLS AND MASCOTS in the dressing room, especially gifts from family or fellow actors.
- SHOES, especially if they squeak on one's first stage entrance.
- CATS, which are lucky backstage.
- COAL, when thrown into the gallery from the stage.
- A RABBIT'S FOOT, traditionally kept in the make-up box.

That actors desire good luck also goes back to the outbreak of the English Civil War in 1642, when theatres were closed and stage players penalized.

for example, devils were dressed in yellow and black to represent the fires of hell. Modern drama, beginning in the Renaissance, is essentially a fusion of the classical and religious forms.

Good luck for an actor centres around the personal – the desire for a performance that commands critical acclaim (and with it the promise of future work) – and for the show, that it may be blessed with good reviews and a long run.

STAGE RIGHT

Like sportsmen and women, thespians set great store by ritual – wearing a lucky costume, garter or socks, or performing certain actions before or during a play. Equally, there are dozens of ways in which bad luck can befall.

Notes and Queries of 1878 perfectly describes a typical good luck ritual of a celebrated actress when she emerged from her dressing room: 'If she met one of the actors … she made him hold up his thumb in front of her; then, placing her thumb on his, she turned her hand round, at the same time pressing downwards. If the thumb on which she pressed held firm she was satisfied, but if it gave way she imagined that she would break down during the performance.'

Many actors will ensure good luck by leaving their dressing room with the left foot first (though a visitor brings good luck by entering right

The nursery rhyme 'Three Blind Mice', which actors regard as extremely unlucky if sung or hummed, especially on opening night, is said to be based on the fates of the Protestant clergymen Latimer, Ridley and Cranmer, who died at the stake. The farmer's wife was Queen Mary I.

foot first) and all consider it highly fortuitous to trip or stumble on stage, especially on an opening night. However, it is courting disaster to have real flowers on stage, to knit on or beside the stage, to whistle in the theatre or to have another actor look over your shoulder while you're putting on your make-up.

ANOTHER 'FATAL' TUNE THAT ACTORS WILL NEVER ALLOW PAST THEIR LIPS IS THAT OF THE SONG 'I DREAMT I DWELT IN MARBLE HALLS' FROM *THE BOHEMIAN GIRL* BY MICHAEL WILLIAM BALFE.

FATED DRAMAS AND LINES

Of all plays, Shakespeare's *Macbeth* (always referred to, for safety's sake, as 'the Scottish play') is most associated with bad luck. Fate also takes a hand in pantomime and in all kinds of theatre sayings and expressions.

It's not known why *Macbeth* should be so unlucky. One theory is that it was regularly staged when audiences were poor and therefore concluded a repertory season. Another is that the witches' song really does cast an evil spell on the play and its actors. Among performances that famously bombed was the 1980 production at London's Old Vic, starring Peter O'Toole. Jack Tinker, writing in the *Daily Mail*, confessed, 'One has to suppress the urge to guffaw.' Not all of the audience did so.

Pantomime began as a Roman entertainment but its modern form is an adaptation of the comic harlequinades of the 1700s. The idea of basing pantomime on fairy tales came late in the 18th century.

The pantomime season is often a vehicle for fading actors down on their luck, though performing *Cinderella* is said to presage a revival in fortunes. But *Robin Hood* and *Babes in the Wood*, while not as unlucky as *Macbeth*, are believed to have bad vibes, especially (as with all plays) if they open on the 13th of the month.

Birds and Animals

All kinds of birds and animals have age-old associations with fortune, and reflect a time when humans were much more closely in touch with the natural world than they are today. Animals were often believed to be gods, goddesses or even witches in disguise and treated accordingly.

WINGED MESSENGERS

'No one knows except some bird' goes the old saying – a tribute to the long-held belief that, because they can fly high in the sky, birds are not only endowed with special powers, both good and bad, but may even be messengers of the gods. In ancient Rome the word *aves* meant both birds and ancestral spirits or ghosts.

By studying the flights, calls and other actions of birds, soothsayers of old used the creatures to read the future and to predict whether it boded good or ill. Generally, it was thought unlucky to see a flock of birds too numerous to count, or to hear a night bird such as an owl calling in the daytime.

That birds may presage death is cemented in a legend that dates back to the 17th century: it is associated with Salisbury Cathedral, where the demise of the bishop is said to be heralded by the appearance of two (unspecified) large white birds, which glide through the air without flapping their wings. Historically, the deaths of both Bishop Moberly in 1885 and Bishop Wordsworth in 1911 are recorded as having been 'announced' in this fashion.

BIRD OMENS

The actions of birds, and the ways we treat them, have ominous messages for the superstitious:

PIGEON .... A pillow stuffed with pigeon feathers protects a person from death.

OWL .... It predicts an unhappy life if it screeches at a child's birth.

LAPWING (PLOVER) ..... Unlucky if seen or caught because it embodies the Devil, hence its cry of 'bewitched, bewitched'.

CUCKOO .... Rolling on your back on the grass two or three times when you hear the first one will protect from backache for the rest of the year.

DOVE .... A harbinger of good news but an omen of death if it flies around your head.

SWALLOW .... A sign of poverty if it perches on the roof.

ROBIN .... If it flies into a church and sings there, it is a 'call of death'.

PROUD AS A PEACOCK

The stately old Spanish dance called the pavan comes from pavones, *the Latin for peacocks. It was so named because its steps demanded that the dancers strut around each other like peacocks.*

Whether or not you regard a peacock as unlucky depends on where you live. In the West they are widely regarded as harbingers of misfortune but in the Orient they are considered to be 'soul birds' and 'paradise birds', which bring good fortune and may raise their voices as oracles.

When approached by a snake or tiger – animals dangerous to humans – or when it is about to rain, the peacock will raise its voice in alarm. Hence its reputation as a foreteller of disaster. This royal bird of medieval England was, in Roman times, sacred to Juno, mother of the gods. The 'eyes' in the bird's tail were symbolic of her watchfulness. After the advent of Christianity the church took over the peacock feather fans, or *flabelli*, used by Juno's priests and priestesses to fan successive popes with the 'many-eyed vigilance of the Church'.

THE PEACOCK FEATURES IN SEVERAL OF AESOP'S *FABLES*, INCLUDING 'THE PEACOCK AND THE MAGPIE' IN WHICH WORTH GETS THE BETTER OF SHOW, AND 'THE PEACOCK'S COMPLAINT' IN WHICH THE BIRD COMPLAINED TO JUNO ABOUT THE COARSENESS OF HIS VOICE IN COMPARISON WITH THAT OF THE NIGHTINGALE. THAT THE GODDESS ASSURED HIM OF HIS BEAUTY LED THE WRITER TO THE MORAL, 'BE CONTENT WITH YOUR LOT'.

The peacock's darker side, particularly the bad luck associated with bringing peacock feathers into the house, or using them on stage in the theatre, comes from its reputation as the bird that consented to show Satan the way to paradise. Even a single feather bearing the bird's 'evil eye' brought indoors can, at best, doom daughters of the house to spinsterhood and at worst bring disaster to the householder.

COILED CHARM

The serpent – the tempter of the Garden of Eden – is a creature revered worldwide for its powers, not always evil ones. Because it regularly sheds its skin the snake was believed by many ancient societies to be an immortal creature that never died of old age.

Ammonites and similar coiled fossils, and other snake-like stones, were once treasured as means of curing illnesses. Legend has it that these objects are created when snakes coil up together and secrete liquid globules, which later solidify.

The links between snakes and immortality are many, and the Genesis story of Adam and Eve has resonances in the Babylonian story of the Great Mother who, attended by a snake, offered man the food of eternal life. Some early Christians even worshipped the serpent, believing it to be an incarnation of Jesus.

In some parts of Britain it is still the custom to kill the first snake you see in spring (which could be a harmless slowworm). This symbolic act, intended to rid a person of their enemies for the rest of the year, is said by some to be especially effective if the creature's head is preserved in a matchbox. According to Hindu tradition, however, vengeance would be wrought on anyone daring to harm the Nagas, the semi-divine 'cobra people' with the bodies of serpents.

TWICE WEEKLY, TO THE ACCOMPANIMENT OF LOUD MUSIC, SOME MEMBERS OF THE PENTECOSTAL HOLINESS CHURCHES OF THE SOUTHERN USA GATHER TO HANDLE POISONOUS SNAKES SUCH AS RATTLESNAKES AND COPPERHEADS, EVEN TOSSING THEM AND WRAPPING THEM AROUND THEIR NECKS, IN THE CONFIDENCE THAT THEIR FAITH WILL PROTECT THEM FROM DANGER. IF BITTEN — WHICH THEY TAKE AS A SIGN OF LAPSED FAITH — FEW SEEK MEDICAL HELP, BELIEVING INSTEAD THAT FAITH WILL CURE THEM. LUCKILY, ATTACKS ARE FEW.

THE WEAVER OF FORTUNE

'If in life you want to thrive, let a spider run alive.' So goes the old saying, which relates to several stories of spiders protecting people. These eight-legged web spinners have for centuries been associated with the weaving of human fates.

Whether your home is in Scotland or the West Indies, killing a spider will, it is said, make you break all your crockery or your wine glasses before the day is out. Another rhyme calls for alternative methods of catching flies: 'Kill a spider and bad luck yours will be,/Until of flies you've swatted fifty-three.'

The duplicity of the spider, with its alluring web, is epitomized in the children's rhyme, written by Mary Howitt in 1829, whose first verse runs:

'Will you walk into my parlour?' said the Spider to the Fly,
'Tis the prettiest little parlour that ever you did spy;
The way into my parlour is up a winding stair,
And I've a many curious things to show when you are there.'
'Oh no, no,' said the little Fly, 'to ask me is in vain,
For who goes up your winding stair can ne'er come down again.'

Lucky Plants

From mighty trees to small plants such as clover, the green world has many links with the preservation and prediction of good fortune, especially at Christmas and other festivals. For flower lovers there is a whole language to be read in their blooms.

FOUR LEAVES FOR LUCK

Finding and keeping a four-leaved clover – or even dreaming of one – has been accepted as a symbol of luck for over 500 years. Since almost all clover leaves have three lobes, there are also special meanings for leaves with five or two.

A five-leaved clover is a sign of great wealth to come. A girl should put a two-leaved clover or 'clover of two' in her right shoe. The first person she meets will be the one she will marry.

For a four-leaved clover to be lucky it must, ideally, be discovered by accident. On the day you find it you may even meet your true love.

The leaves of fortune are naturally produced most often by the white clover, (*Trifolium repens*) also known, from its colour, as milky blobs. Some also call it bee-bread on account of the fact – well known to country children – that if you pull a slender flower from the round head and suck its base you will get a *soupçon* of honey.

To prolong the luck a four-leaved clover confers, which includes being able to see through malign tricks and to see and avoid evil spirits, the leaf should be pressed and is believed to have the most beneficial effects if kept in a prayer book or Bible. Should you dream of a four-leaved clover your luck will follow the tenets of this rhyme:

As if to contrive good luck, four-leaved clovers are commercially grown and sold by the thousand, particularly in the USA.

One leaf for fame, one leaf for wealth,
One leaf for a faithful lover,
And one leaf to bring glorious health –
All are in the four-leaved clover.

THE POWER OF TREES

Our ancestors' veneration for trees probably comes from the fact that they are so long-lived, outliving many human generations. Some trees were believed to protect against evil and to cure illnesses, especially in children.

The ancient Celts divided the year into four segments, each designated by a tree. Oak marked the spring equinox, birch the summer solstice and olive the autumn equinox. Beech was the tree of the winter solstice, but the night of 21–22 December was known as the night of the silver fir, when fir logs – the original Yule logs – were burnt.

To the Greeks, certain trees were not only sacred but ascribed to specific deities. The laurel, for instance, was sacred to Apollo, the god of light, music, medicine and prophecy, and branches of

TREE LORE

Be careful how you treat trees, they may have a significant effect on your life:

- OAK Damaging the tree brings bad luck. Sitting beneath it protects from witches and evil spirits.
- ELDER Burning elder or 'witch wood' in the fire in the hearth brings death to a house.
- HAWTHORN Don't sit beneath a hawthorn on May Day, Midsummer's Eve or Halloween or you may become enchanted by fairies.
- OLIVE Protects against witchcraft and lightning.
- WILLOW A child beaten with a willow stick will stop growing. The weeping willow symbolizes sadness.
- BIRCH Brings luck and averts the evil eye. Put birch branches over a baby's cradle for protection.
- MAPLE Passing a child through maple branches will bring long life.
- MONKEY PUZZLE If you talk as you pass the tree you'll have bad luck for three years, but when planted in a graveyard it keeps the Devil at bay.

the tree were ceremonially brought to his temple at Delphi. To appease the gods, it was the custom to hang sacred trees with the spoils of the chase and the arms of conquerors.

THE CONCEPT OF THE TREE AS REPRESENTATIVE OF THE UNIVERSE IS COMMON TO MANY DIFFERENT CULTURES. THE TREE OF KNOWLEDGE APPEARS BOTH IN THE BIBLICAL GARDEN OF EDEN, WHERE ITS FRUIT TEMPTED ADAM AND EVE, AND IN THE GREEK GARDEN OF THE HESPERIDES, WHERE ITS FRUITS MAINTAINED THE IMMORTALITY OF THE GODS. YGGDRASIL, THE NORSE WORLD TREE, HAD ITS ROOTS IN THE UNDERWORLD AND ITS CROWN IN THE HEAVENS.

MAGICAL EVERGREENS

Because they do not lose their leaves with the seasons, evergreens have long been symbols of immortality, used in celebrations and festivals. Many people are still highly superstitious about harming such trees.

According to Greek legend, the nymph Daphne, when pursued by the god Apollo, was transformed by the gods into a laurel. The tree, also known as sweet bay (*Laurus nobilis*), was subsequently commanded by Apollo to bear its leaves in both summer and winter. He also ordained that they be used to 'crown all who excelled in courage, service, or the creation of beauty', a tradition carried on to this day and watched by millions at the Athens Olympiad of 2004. Placing laurel leaves under the pillow of someone striving to be a poet was believed to have the magical effect of bringing inspiration.

The yew was part of the witches' brew in Shakespeare's Macbeth, *specifically 'Gall of goat, and slips of yew/Sliver'd [broken] in the moon's eclipse.' Because the yew protects against evil it is extremely unlucky to break a yew branch, and one such is thought dangerous to use.*

The yew (*Taxus baccata*) is not only long-lived – individual trees are believed to have lived 3,000 years and more – but also an ancient symbol of life

Baccalaureate, a word derived from the Latin for 'bachelor', includes a punning reference to the berry (baca) of the laurel (laureus), alluding to the bay wreaths worn by scholars receiving academic honours.

after death. Since mourners have, for centuries, carried yew branches at funerals it is no coincidence that ancient yew trees are a common sight in old churchyards. As well as preventing witches from approaching the church, the trees were thought to 'attract and imbibe putrefaction and gross oleaginous vapours exhaled from the graves'.

BLOSSOMS OF DOOM?

Though flowers will beautify any home, be careful which blooms you bring into the house or you may introduce evil spirits. The superstitious also choose their garden plants with care, though even the most diligent gardener cannot stop them blooming at the wrong time of year and so invoking bad luck.

Of all the unlucky flowers, hawthorn or may brought indoors has the most malign reputation and is said to portend death, especially of the mother of the house. The tree (*Crataegus monogyna*) blooms around

While finding the first daffodil in spring is an omen of wealth in the year to come, it is very unlucky if its head hangs towards you. Such are the contradictions of superstition!

the time of Beltane, the Celtic festival that coincides with May Day (see p 47). Before the Reformation, people would make 'May altars' – statues of the Virgin Mary surrounded with may blossom – to deter witches for a twelvemonth. After it, when the mass was forbidden in England and priests were in mortal danger, Roman Catholics would put sprigs of may blossom in their windows as secret signs that the priest would be saying mass there – another explanation of the superstition that it can presage disaster.

No superstitious person would pick a foxglove and bring it into the house or take it on to a ship. Daffodils are also deemed to deter the hatching of the eggs of geese and chickens, while apple blossom will, it's said, bring sickness with it into the house. A single snowdrop, said to look like a corpse in its shroud, has long been considered a 'death token', but a bunch of blooms may, some say, break the spell.

FLOWER SIGNS AND SUPERSTITIONS
The meanings behind some garden blooms:

ROSE	If it blooms in autumn it means misfortune the following year.
SUNFLOWER	Good luck to plant.
FOXGLOVE	Unlucky to transplant.
LILY OF THE VALLEY	Unlucky to plant.
LILAC	Lucky to find a five-petalled blossom.
PRIMROSE	Unlucky if it flowers unseasonably.
VIOLET	A death omen if it flowers in the autumn.
HOUSELEEK	Protects a home if grown on the roof.
HYDRANGEA	Grown near the house it will prevent daughters from marrying.

Festive Fortune

Special times of year bring with them not only traditional rituals but the particular need for good fortune, both on the day and in the months to come. That many religious festivals were borrowed and adapted from pagan traditions underlines the folklore behind well-known and much-loved customs.

RING IN THE NEW

Banishing the old year, and giving a proper welcome to the new one on 1 January, is the time-honoured way to ensure good fortune for the months ahead. And your actions and resolutions at New Year will set the precedent for the future.

In the Middle Ages New Year was celebrated on 25 March, the time of Easter, and was a season of atonement, more like the Jewish Yom Kippur.

New Year celebrations began as a midwinter rite which involved the killing of the king of the old year – often symbolized by a sacrificed animal – and his replacement with a new monarch destined to ensure the return of spring and a fruitful season. Malevolent spirits were chased away with loud noises, often including the beating of cow hides with sticks. The tradition persists today in the ringing of church bells, raucous party revelry and (especially in Scotland where New Year or Hogmanay is the year's best-loved celebration) the singing of Robert Burns's 'Auld Lang Syne'.

According to Armenian-American folklore, all rivers and springs stop flowing for five minutes after the stroke on midnight on New Year's Eve. If you happen to be at a spring when it starts flowing again you will find, for a few moments, gold dust pouring from the ground.

As the doors of the house are thrown open at midnight to 'let out the old' it is unlucky to take anything out before something is brought in. Enter the first footer, who for the best of fortune should have dark hair, carry a lump of coal to keep the fire going, ring the doorbell, then enter through the back door and leave by the front.

CHINESE NEW YEAR

Timed to begin at the new moon closest to the beginning of spring (halfway between the winter solstice and the spring equinox), the Chinese New Year falls between 21 January and 19 February. Central to the celebrations is paying homage to the ancestors.

To ensure that all his reports to the heavenly Jade Emperor are sweet, it is customary at Chinese New Year – also known as the Spring Festival – to smear honey over a statuette of the kitchen god

Firecrackers are set off at New Year to draw the attention of the gods to the people and, as in the West, to scare away evil spirits.

Zao Wang. The kitchen is a hive of activity in the run-up to the New Year, because it is deemed unlucky to work during the first few days of the celebrations, or to use knives or scissors in case they sever good fortune. Symbolizing family unity, the main domestic event of the festival is a meal at which a whole fish is served. New Year is also an auspicious time for weddings.

The 'thousand layer' sweet cake made with rice flour and eaten at Chinese New Year is a symbol of longevity.

Because they believe it is unlucky to enter the New Year with dust from the past clinging to them, the Chinese routinely pay off their debts and clean out their houses at the end of the old year – sweeping at New Year sweeps away good luck. These days, however, if anyone is unable to pay their dues they are no longer morally obliged to kill themselves at the year's end, as was deemed necessary in the past.

THE LION DANCE PERFORMED IN CHINESE COMMUNITIES WORLDWIDE PAYS TRIBUTE TO THE BUDDHIST SYMBOL OF COURAGE, CONSTANCY AND MAJESTY. THE LION DANCES IN FRONT OF EVERY DOOR TO BRING GOOD LUCK, TO THE ACCOMPANIMENT OF THE NOISE OF DRUMS, CYMBALS AND FIRECRACKERS.

EASTER PARADE

New clothes are believed to bring good fortune for the year. The new hat or Easter bonnet became even more popular after the release of the 1948 film Easter Parade, *starring Fred Astaire and Judy Garland.*

Easter, the Christian festival of the Resurrection and the Church's holiest day, also relates to pagan rites of spring. Its many rituals and symbols, from wearing new clothes to hunting for Easter eggs, underline its significance to fertility and the promise of new life.

It has long been believed that when the sun rises on Easter morning it dances for joy. Luckiest of all is to see its movements reflected in a mirror or in water. As Francis Kilvert, writing in his diary on

14 October 1870, says: 'To this pool the people used to come on Easter morning to see the sun dance and play in the water and the angels who were at the Resurrection playing backwards and forwards before the sun.' Luckiest of all is to see a lamb (the symbol of Christ) in the sun's centre.

The association between eggs and rebirth is obvious, and in some ancient cultures the earth is believed to have 'hatched' from a cosmic egg. In many places hens' eggs are still painted red at Easter to symbolize bloodshed. Children are believed to be especially blessed when they eat the eggs they have hunted for on Easter Day.

In Scandinavia 'wise women' would chant rhymes to rid the home of unfriendly Easter elves. However, the benign 'household brownies' would have food put out for them to make sure they not only stayed all summer but brought good fortune with them.

TRICKS, TREATS AND SOULS DEPARTED

Halloween, the eve of All Saint's Day or All Hallows, is a night of magic charms and divinations from the dead. Once witches and ghosts had to be propitiated, a belief played out today in 'trick-or-treating'.

Halloween, the festival of the dead, was originally adopted from Samhain, the Celtic feast marking the end of summer. Its name may be derived from Samana, the god of death, or from a Gaelic word that simply means 'summer's end'. On this night the veil between the worlds of the living and the dead was thought to be at its thinnest; the spirits of the dead were believed to make themselves visible to humans and walk the earth, while the pagan gods played tricks on people everywhere. The many traditional ways of allaying the effects of evil on Halloween, particularly preventing the dead returning in malign form, include ducking for apples – catching apples floating in a tub of water solely with your teeth. In Irish lore, the apples are said to represent the souls contained in the 'cauldron of regeneration'.

Like Midsummer, this is a time for seeing your future lover (see p 50). And according to Sicilian tradition, children are given gifts at Halloween because this is when dead relatives become 'good fairies of the little ones'. This children's rhyme is a favourite with Mexican children; they chant it as they go from house to house:

Let's pray, let's pray
We are little angels,
From heaven we come.
If you don't give to us
Your doors and windows
We will break.

MORE HALLOWEEN CUSTOMS
Time-honoured beliefs affecting fortune:

* Make sheep and lambs pass through a hoop of rowan (mountain ash) branches.
* At sea, throw a cup of ale into the water to enrich the catch.
* Take food to a cemetery and leave it to feed dead souls.
* If, on Halloween, you catch a falling leaf before it reaches the ground you can have a wish.
* Take and mark an ivy leaf for each member of the family and float them on a bowl of water overnight. If a coffin symbol appears, that indicates a death within the year.

LIGHT IN THE WORLD

**As the days grow shorter and the year reaches its end,
the tradition in many cultures is to hold festivals of light.**
**Among the many rituals played out are those
intended to ensure the return of spring and a
lucky year ahead.**

*In the eight-day Jewish
festival of Hanukkah
one candle is lit on
the first night, two on
the second and so on.
It commemorates the
rededication of the
Temple in Jerusalem
after its desecration
by foreign forces.
The celebration also
reaffirms the continuing
struggle of the faithful
to live by God's
commandments.*

In the 4th century, St Ambrose, Bishop of Milan,
said of Christmas: 'Well do Christian people call
this holy day, on which Our Lord was born, the
day of the new Sun.' He neatly summed up the
fact that to celebrate the nativity the early Church
had hijacked the ancient custom of worshipping
Mithras, the Persian god of light and guardian
against evil. Also absorbed into Christmas were
the bawdy Roman feast of Saturnalia, celebrated
in mid-December, and the northern European
Yule, an occasion when homes were brightly lit and
decorated with evergreens – both of them symbols
of renewal and eternal life.

A variety of superstitions are associated with
these Christmas symbols. Pieces of candle lit on the evening
of Christmas Eve must be allowed, for luck, to burn all night.
These candles must be snuffed – never blown – out and a piece
of the candle end, or at the very least a piece of the wick, must
be kept for good fortune. Equally, it is unlucky to stir the Yule
log on the fire on Christmas Eve, and keeping a piece of the log
to light the fire in the coming year will ensure good fortune.

DIWALI, THE WEEK-LONG HINDU FESTIVAL OF LIGHTS, IS ALSO A NEW
YEAR CELEBRATION AND A COMMEMORATION OF THE DAY ON WHICH
LORD RAMA, AN INCARNATION OF VISHNU, HAVING DEFEATED THE
TEN-HEADED DEMON RAVANA, RETURNED TO HIS KINGDOM. SYMBOLI-
CALLY, IT ACKNOWLEDGES THE TRIUMPH OF LIGHT OVER DARKNESS,
TRUTH OVER FALSEHOOD AND SPIRITUALITY OVER IMMORALITY.

DECORATED WITH CARE

The business of Christmas decorations – particularly where they are put and when they are taken down – is a matter of importance when it comes to luck. Christmas food is also the subject of firmly held beliefs passed down through the generations.

Though for many people in Europe the annual arrival of St Nicholas with his gifts on 6 December marks the beginning of the Christmas season, many hold that evergreen decorations should not be put up until Christmas Eve. As well as holly, ivy and mistletoe (see p 51), laurel, rosemary, box and bay have all been used over the centuries, but never yew, which is believed to presage a death in the family. And ivy must always be mixed with other plants for it is said to be 'a plant of bad omen' that 'will prove injurious'.

The Christmas tree, traditionally a fir, became popular in the 19th century thanks to Queen Victoria's consort Prince Albert, but as a symbol of enduring life, the decorated evergreen bough can be traced to the midwinter celebrations of the Middle Ages and may go as far back as the Iron Age.

Keep your decorations in place beyond Twelfth Night (6 January) and ill luck will befall. That's the popular belief, though in former times they were often left until Candlemas – on 2 February. It was the custom in many places to burn the decorations, either at home or on communal bonfires. If they were simply thrown out of the house it was feared there would be a death in the family. However, the ivy was sometimes fed to milking cows to increase their yield.

Body Power

If luck is with us it may be, so tradition dictates, that it is somehow expressed by and within our bodies. As well as palm reading, other features have long been used to foretell the future, from the shapes of hands, ears and eyebrows to the positioning of dimples.

THE EYES OF FORTUNE

The eyes – the windows of the soul – are the mirrors, for good or bad, of our own and others' thoughts and feelings. And it is as well to know how to deal effectively with the malign influence of the 'evil eye'.

What makes the eyes so important as symbols of power is their ability to influence what they see. In ancient Egypt it was

> *It is said that if your right eye itches you will cry, if your left one does so you will laugh, though in some places the predictions are reversed and 'Left or right brings good at night' – so believe what you will.*

common to wear an amulet called an Uzat-eye, or 'eye of Horus', usually made of precious metal. This endowed its wearer with the strength of the life-giving sun and gave protection against the evil eye, which, by contrast, brings misfortune or illness, or destroys all it looks on – which explains why newborn babies were once plastered with mud or soot to disguise and thus protect them.

While such malignity was often deliberate, it was not always so. There are well-documented accounts of those said to be cursed with the evil eye, such as a man described in *About Yorkshire* in 1883, who 'always walked about with his eyes fixed on the ground, and never looked at any one to whom he spoke; his glance was cursed, and he dare not speak to one of the rosy children, lest some blight should fall upon it.' Witches, like Nanny Morgan the Shropshire woman murdered in 1857, were commonly thought to be possessed of the evil eye.

EYEBROWS THAT MEET IN THE MIDDLE HAVE LONG ASSOCIATIONS WITH, AT BEST, DECEITFULNESS AND, AT WORST, THE EVIL EYE. AS ONE VICTORIAN JINGLE RUNS: 'TRUST NOT THE MAN WHOSE EYEBROWS MEET,/FOR IN HIS HEART YOU'LL FIND DECEIT.'

FACE THE FACTS?

Our front to the world, the face is our most important means of expression. So it is not surprising that as well as the eyes, virtually every feature of the face is the subject of some kind of lore, relating to both sensation and shape.

Shape is important for both cheeks and chin, where dimples can occur. However, there is no consensus as to whether dimples are lucky or not, as these rhymes suggest:

Dimple on the chin.
The Devil within,
Dimple on the cheek,
A soul mild and meek.

Alternatively when wealth is at stake:

Dimple in your chin,
Your living's brought in,
Dimple in your cheek.
Your living's to seek.

Regarding facial sensations, nature and position are critical to interpretation. If your cheeks or ears tingle or burn, someone is talking about you. For the ears such talk is good if it affects your right ear, bad if it affects the left. Ringing in the ears, however, is generally considered to be a bad omen, even a kind of 'death peal'. Tingling lips mean that someone will kiss you soon. An itching right eye is a sign that you will soon see the one you love.

CHARACTER READING

It's said by many that you can read a person's character from the size and shape of their features, for instance:

ROUNDED CHEEKS	Lively, wise
HOLLOW CHEEKS	Mean, cold
LARGE EARS	Generous, intelligent
SMALL EARS	Instinctive, mean
POINTED EARS	Artful, conniving
ARCHED EYEBROWS	Imaginative
STRAIGHT EYEBROWS	Alert, wary
THIN LIPS	Unemotional
FULL LIPS	Pleasure-loving

HAIR MATTERS

Its colour, treatment and even the way it grows – and in what profusion – are all significant as far as hair is concerned. And, by tradition, you should be careful what you do with shed hair, whether it's cut or comes out naturally on the brush or comb.

When discarded hair is thrown into the flames, watch how it burns. The brighter the flame, the longer the life. Before doing so, you can also perform a character test. Pull a strand of hair sharply between the nails of forefinger and thumb. If it curls up after it is released then you are deemed to be either consumed with pride or to lack faithfulness as a lover.

Though (except for the bald) we each have, on average, some 100,000 hairs on our head, the way they grow can vary enormously. A lucky 'double crown' or double parting will help endow its owner with either a long life, riches, or both. A widow's peak, in which a woman's hair grows in a point low down on her forehead, is a sign that she will outlive her husband.

For safety, it has long been common practice to dispose of hair combings and cuttings by burning them, lest they fall into the wrong hands. If left lying about unattended and picked up by a bird they could be woven into a nest and cause their original owner endless headaches. And if the bird that steals them is a magpie, then death could ensue within the year. Worst of all is for hair to be stolen by a witch and added to her witch bottle – a collection of items used for casting spells.

BALDNESS IS THE GENETIC FATE OF MANY MEN, AND A FEW WOMEN. FOLK REMEDIES FOR CURING BALDNESS – NONE OF WHICH HAVE MUCH CREDENCE – INCLUDE RUBBING GOOSE DUNG, FOX FAT, ONION JUICE OR BEAR FAT MIXED WITH LAUDANUM INTO THE SCALP. TO PREVENT BALDNESS OLD WIVES' RECOMMENDATIONS ARE TO STAND BAREHEADED IN THE RAIN AND ALWAYS AVOID HATS THAT ARE TOO TIGHT.

THE HAND OF FATE

A gruesome charm long used by both burglars and sorcerers was the Hand of Glory. While the body of a condemned man was still hanging on the gibbet the hand was cut off, pickled and dried, and a lighted candle was placed in it. This, thieves believed, would prevent people from waking while they were being robbed.

From Old Testament times, when the prophets believed that God 'set his seal' on humans by imprinting it on their hands, people have attempted to read not only a person's character, but also their fate, from the hands and fingers.

The human hand, with its opposable thumb and index finger, is the evolutionary asset that has made us toolmakers par excellence. And while the hand can be used as a powerful weapon, its healing touch is the gentlest of strokes.

The hand is raised in blessing and shaken in friendly greeting. An open hand, symbolized for

HAND MEANINGS

Some common interpretations of shapes:

HANDS

LONG AND SLENDER	Fastidious, gentle
THIN, DRY	Nervous, touchy, tenacious
LARGE AND STRAIGHT	Lively, expansive, possibly aggressive
HARD AND FIRM	Energetic, with a good memory
HOT	Vigorous but possibly insincere
COLD	Taciturn but secretly generous

FINGERS AND THUMB

LARGE THUMB	Strong-minded, self-controlled
LONG FINGERS	Polite, anxious, delicate
SHORT FINGERS	Impatient, sensuous, creative
POINTED FINGERS	Impatient, creative, illogical

millennia in protective amulets, is an ancient guard against the evil eye (see p 147). The malignant power of the evil eye can also be warded off by holding the hand with the two middle fingers and thumb bent inwards and the index and little fingers extended like horns.

Luck, it is said, will rub off if you stroke the hand of a fortunate person, but it is believed to be unlucky to wash your hands in the same bowl of water as someone else; a quarrel is sure to ensue. If your left palm itches then rub it on wood or you will soon lose your money. An itching right palm however, is a sign that either money, good news or both are on their way to you.

TOOTH POWER

Ever since our ancient ancestors wore strings of wild animals' teeth around their necks to endow them with strength and aggression in the hunt, teeth have been symbols of energy. To dream of losing your teeth is commonly interpreted as a sign of deep depression, and can even be an omen of death.

Teeth both in and out of the mouth are subject to superstitious beliefs. For a baby to be born with one or more teeth, or have them erupt earlier than normal (especially if the upper ones appear first) is not propitious for, as the 17th-century proverb runs: 'Soon toothed, soon with God.' Equally, both violence and intelligence are also associated with early teething. A short life has often been linked with having a wide gap between the front teeth, though prosperity is the more usual prognosis. Today's children leave their shed teeth under the pillow, hoping for a monetary exchange with the 'tooth fairy', but in former times it was the custom for the teeth to be sprinkled with salt and burnt in the fire while saying the rhyme: 'Old tooth, new tooth/Pray God send me a good tooth.' The reason for such treatment was to prevent animals getting hold of shed teeth – in which case, it was believed, the new one would grow like the tooth of the animal that stole it – or to ensure that it was not procured by a witch and used to wreak evil on its original owner.

For adults, fallen or extracted teeth were burned in the same way as milk teeth, primarily to avert witchcraft. Even into the 20th century they were often kept carefully until death and buried with a corpse so that the body of the departed could be considered 'complete'. Teeth were customarily placed in the hand so that, on reaching Heaven, the dead could easily account for every tooth in their heads.

A prayer-come-rhyme used as a charm and recorded in the 1890s even invoked the mighty powers:

Peter was sitting on a marble stone
And Jesus passed by:
Peter said, 'My Lord! My God!
How my tooth doth ache!'
Jesus said, 'Peter art whole!
And whosoever keeps these words for
*   my sake*
Shall never have the toothache.' Amen.

Teeth ache when worn down by decay, which exposes their sensitive, nerve-rich roots. Before the days of anaesthetics, when bad teeth were roughly and painfully pulled, charms for keeping teeth pain-free were welcomed. Wearing a tooth from a dead person's skull or a mole's foot around the neck were supposed to keep toothache at bay.

Fortune's Rainbow

Colours in general, and the colours of many specific objects, are the subjects of various superstitions, such as the practice of choosing pink for a girl and blue for a boy, or dressing by the maxim that 'red and green should never be seen'.

THE COLOURS OF LUCK

Of all the colours in the rainbow, green, blue and red are the ones most associated with superstitions – plus the 'non-colours' black and white. But the best way to use colours to good effect is probably to employ them according to the established principles of colour psychology to enhance your mood.

When it comes to choosing a car colour, set superstition aside in favour of statistics. Pale colours are safer than dark ones and silver the safest of all, giving 50 per cent more 'protection' to drivers than white.

Pick your colour according to your needs and you will feel better. Yellow and orange, for instance, are hues to boost your optimism and self-confidence. In ancient times, these 'sun colours' were associated with the beneficial forces of light and the celebration of victory. Red, as well as its romantic associations with hearts and flowers (see p 30), is the colour of energy and of life-giving blood. Used as the colour of a talisman, red will, it's said, protect against both witches and the Devil.

THE COLOUR OF FORTUNE
Your lucky colour, according to astrologers,
depends on the star sign under which you were born:

ARIES .... Red, black, white
TAURUS .... Blue, pastel shades
GEMINI .... Orange
CANCER .... Yellow, orange, indigo
LEO .... Yellow and orange
VIRGO .... Brown, cream, acid green
LIBRA .... Green, purple, pink
SCORPIO .... Deep red, blue-green
SAGITTARIUS.. Blue, purple, white
CAPRICORN .... Green-grey, indigo, violet
AQUARIUS.. Violet, pale yellow
PISCES .... Violet, pale green, blue

IN BLACK AND WHITE

Often, but by no means always, white plays good against black's evil, but the fortunes of these two 'colours' may change with tradition and culture. So while black is the shade for mourning in the Christian tradition, white is chosen, for purity, as the colour for the shroud.

The negative connotations of black derive from its association with darkness, or absence of light, but to the ancient Egyptians it was linked with fertility – as the colour of both the soil and clouds heavy with life-giving rain. And while bad things happen on Black Mondays, the Black Death wiped out up to a third of the population and black sheep bring shame on families, it's black cats that are widely

White, in the white feather and the white flag, is the colour of cowardice, shame and surrender.

thought of as lucky (except if they cross your path in the USA or Europe) as are black dogs and hares.

White, the absence of colour, may be associated with such unsullied items as snow and milk, although giving white flowers, especially lilies or white lilac, to a sick person is said to be the surest way of hastening their demise. White birds have a special symbolism. If they fly into a mine they are thought to be harbingers of disaster, but it is lucky to encounter a white cockerel. To Muslims the White Bird represents the soul or conscience; to them the souls of the just lie, like white birds, beneath God's throne.

That a prism will split white light into the colours of the rainbow was the discovery of Isaac Newton during his experiments in the 1660s. It was previously thought that colours were mixtures of light and darkness in different proportions.

BLUE FOR YOU

Blue, the colour of the sea and sky – the poet Shelley's 'overhanging heaven' – is the colour of truth and, in the Chinese tradition, of scholarship and also spiritual knowledge. In both colour therapy and Jungian psychology, blue is the colour of calm.

Since the ancient Greeks associated blue with Zeus, father of the gods, blue has been a propitious colour, worn by royalty and, iconically, the

Whether ancient Britons really coloured their skin blue with woad (Isatis tinctoria) is a matter of conjecture although it is mentioned in Caesar's De Bello Gallico. The plant was certainly used for centuries as a dye until superseded by indigo.

Virgin Mary. Blue will, it is said, defuse the power of the evil eye. That the children of Israel fringed their clothes with 'a ribband of blue' is another reason why blue clothes are thought to be lucky for all and obligatory for happy brides.

Blue was worn by royalty until it was superseded by red and purple, but symbolizes the best of the best in the form of the blue ribbon. Even touching something blue may make wishes come true, and an old cure for cramp in cattle was to rub their legs with a milkmaid's blue bonnet.

FEELING DOWN? BLUE IS THE COLOUR OF DEPRESSION AND OF THE MUSIC BORN OF AMERICAN SLAVERY, THOUGH AS ONE MAN BORN IN NEW ORLEANS IN THE 1860s ATTESTED, 'THE BLUES WAS HERE WHEN I COME.' EARLY BLUES OWED MUCH TO WORK SONGS, VERY OFTEN BEGINNING WITH THE PHRASE 'I WOKE UP ONE MORNING …'

GREEN AS GRASS

Most closely associated with foliage, green is the colour of life and the Resurrection. It can also be malign, whether in envy – the 'green-eyed monster' – or when worn at a wedding.

Green, the colour of the planet Venus, is a colour of love and has not always been bad luck for brides: it is worn by the bride in Jan van Eyck's highly symbolic portrait of *Giovanni Arnolfini and his Wife* (1434), and was favoured until the 19th century, presumably because of its links with fertility. For the same reason, evergreens are lucky plants for Christmas decorations (see p 146). Less propitiously, green was the colour of the fairies.

Natural phenomena may be deemed fortunate when linked with green. A wish made at the instant when the green flash is seen (if you are lucky) on the horizon immediately after the sun

If you're lucky with your health you may live to a 'green old age', with all the experience a 'greenhorn' lacks. Fortune may also endow you with green fingers or thumbs, making you adept at growing everything from green peas to greengages.

> THE GREEN MAN OR JACK IN THE GREEN WAS PLAYED BY A BOY
> WHO CAMOUFLAGED HIMSELF IN A WOODEN FRAME DECKED WITH
> BOUGHS AND OTHER GREENERY AND TOOK PART IN FESTIVALS SUCH
> AS MAY DAY AND OTHER COUNTRY RITES. ALTHOUGH SOME BELIEVE
> HIS PURPOSE WAS TO ENSURE THE FERTILITY OF THE YOUNG, OTHERS
> REGARD THE GREEN MAN AS A SINISTER CHARACTER AND POSSIBLY
> EVEN AN INCARNATION OF THE DEVIL HIMSELF.

has set is one that is believed to come true. But a green moon is a sign of foreboding. After the catastrophic eruption of the volcano Krakatoa in 1883 the moon turned green – probably because ash particles lingering in the air scattered the light.

Worn and Carried

For the superstitious, it matters what you wear and how you wear it. By tradition there are special days for donning new clothes, and strict rules for what to do with the old ones. It is also important to be careful what you put in your pockets and what you carry with you, especially on journeys.

To attract the best of fortune you should, said the stoic philosopher Epictetus, 'Know, first, who you are; and then adorn yourself accordingly.'

DRESSING FOR FORTUNE

Be wary about how you get dressed in the morning – it could affect your whole day. Equally, it is deemed very unlucky to mend a torn garment without taking it off first.

Accidentally put a garment on inside out when you're dressing and, it's said, you should keep it like that all day or your luck will change for the worse. If, however, you do your buttons up wrongly then to avoid ill fortune you should correct the mistake right away.

'Something new' is not just a maxim for a bride but also for Easter. Wearing old clothes on Easter day will, according to country lore, attract the foul attentions of crows. New clothes are also symbolic of the new start that the Easter message promises. You don't need an entirely new outfit. Gloves, scarf or a new 'Easter bonnet' will do. An old English custom is to pinch someone wearing new clothes 'for luck'. New clothes and shoes are also customary at the Jewish Passover festival. '*Tischadesh*', meaning 'Wear it in good health', is a favoured greeting to someone so dressed.

BEWARE OF GIVING YOUR CAST-OFF CLOTHES TO A TRAMP OR BEGGAR — UNLESS SUCH INDIVIDUALS ARE WELL KNOWN TO YOU. THIS SUPERSTITION STEMS FROM THE FEAR THAT ANY STRANGER, BUT PARTICULARLY ONE IN DIRE CIRCUMSTANCES, MIGHT BE A WITCH IN DISGUISE AND IN TAKING YOUR CLOTHES COULD CAST AN EVIL SPELL ON YOU IN RETURN.

SAFETY IN YOUR POCKET

To keep you safe from danger, and especially to avoid the influences of the evil eye, it has long been customary to carry or wear an amulet – a charm endowed with a magic power. Both the substance of the amulet and any engravings it bears are critical to its effectiveness.

Materials used for amulets can vary hugely. As well as animal parts and shapes they can consist of anything, such as the grass and stone favoured by native Americans. Precious stones (especially astrological birthstones) are popular and are often set

> *For jewellery, coral beads are thought to confer great protection, which is why they are favoured as christening gifts for girl babies. Charm bracelets are also popular and may include symbols such as the acorn for youthfulness and vigour.*

into rings. Amulet metals can range from the iron favoured for horseshoes through lead to gold and silver.

Certain shapes have particular resonances. The five-pointed star or pentacle, known in medieval times as the Wizard's Star, was emblematic of the mysteries of the universe and was believed to strengthen the soul. The crescent moon shape is believed to confer special luck on lovers and travellers, while wearing the three charms of a cross for faith, an anchor for hope and a heart for charity (love) all together is an old way of receiving protection from all kinds of evil.

ANIMAL AMULETS

From rabbits' feet to silver pigs, animals feature strongly in amulets from all over the world. Their power is generally thought to derive from the lucky associations of the creature concerned.

The cat, sacred to the Egyptians, was popular with them as both an amulet and as a mascot to be taken into battle with their warriors to ensure victory. Though despised in medieval times as a witches' familiar, the cat is still highly regarded as fortunate, not least because of its legendary 'nine lives'. Also favoured

> *The rabbit's foot is commonly used in the voodoo rituals brought to the island of Haiti by slaves from the Yoruba and other African peoples. The word 'voodoo', and its synonym 'hoodoo', mean a malevolent magical force, though 'hoodoo man' is a term for a conjuror.*

by the Egyptians was the scarab or dung beetle, which symbolized the power of the sun because the beetle lays its eggs in dung and they hatch when warmed by sunlight.

In 'Good Luck Charm', his 1962 hit written by Aaron Schroeder and Wally Gold, Elvis Presley famously sang that he could do without a rabbit's foot. He was after a different kind of good luck charm to hang on his arm that 'no rabbit's foot can bring'.

While an amulet can be thought of as passive, a talisman is effective only when its owner interacts with it in some way, for instance by waving, touching or kissing it.

ANIMAL LUCK
Other animal and bird symbols used on amulets:

EAGLE .... Will help you rise in life. It was used as a symbol by the Roman legions and Napoleon's Army and is also a popular symbol in China and Japan.

FISH .... A sign of wealth and fertility. Ideally when used as an amulet it should be in gold or mother of pearl. In Japan it is thought to bring courage.

LADYBIRD (LADYBUG) .... Brings good fortune. As an amulet it should be made of gold.

OWL .... Bringer of knowledge and sagacity.

PIG .... Confers good health, especially if it is a silver amulet.

Forces of Good and Evil

The worst of ill fortune is brought to us by evil incarnations – from malign elves to witches and their accompanying familiars. For many, protection from malign influences comes in the form of good fairies and, especially, guardian angels.

TO WATCH OVER YOU

Biblically, the original role of angels was as divine messenger, representation of both the voice and hand of God. Though not strictly an article of faith, the idea that every individual soul has a guardian angel to watch over them is, as St Jerome said, 'the mind of the Church'. But angels do not always act as forces for good; they can sometimes bring destruction in their wake.

Fortune reversed: fallen angels are those sentenced to hell for sins such as pride or lust, where they take on the form of Satan or the Devil and his demons. In Jewish lore the fallen angel Mastema was the chief of evil spirits. His name means 'hatred' and as well as trying to kill Moses it was Mastema who hardened the Pharaoh's heart against the Israelites.

Even before the Christian era, peoples such as the Babylonians and Assyrians believed in the concept of the guardian angel. Not only are they depicted in sculptures, but Nabopolassar, king of Babylon and father of Nebuchadnezzar, is recorded as having '… a tutelary deity [cherub] of grace to go at my side; in everything that I did, he made my work to succeed.'

In the Bible, guardian angels are evident in many roles. In the Old Testament angels are given the power to discern good and evil, have all-knowing wisdom and the certainty of always making the right choices. It was an angel who led the Israelites in their Exodus from Egypt and another who, at a call from heaven, restrained Abraham from killing his son Isaac. In the New Testament guardian angels appear with equal regularity, succouring

Christ in the Garden of Gethsemane and delivering St Peter from prison.

One of the most powerful Bible passages relating to guardian angels is in Genesis, where Jacob, blessing Joseph's sons, says: '... the God who has been my shepherd all my life to this day, the angel who rescued me from all misfortune, may he bless these boys; they will be called by my name, and by the names of my forefathers, Abraham and Isaac; may they grow into a great people on earth.'

FACING THE DEMONS

If ill fortune comes your way and your sleep is filled with nightmares then, so the annals of witchcraft maintain, you may be troubled by demons. These 'servants of the Devil' may take the form of imps or witches' familiars, or may even become manifest as poltergeists.

As conventionally pictured in art through the ages, demons are miniature versions of the Devil, complete with horns and wings, blackened skin and cloven feet, though they are also believed to be able to take on, at will, all kinds of different disguises. Flying at night they can not only disturb people's dreams but may take over or possess their bodies to such an extent that only exorcism will remove them.

How do demons find their way into the body? According to tradition by 'any unguarded orifice' or by trickery. A witch's familiar might infect her victim by offering an infected food – often an apple – to her victim.

The cunning of demons, and the reasons for avoiding or defending yourself against them were clearly expressed by the French lawyer and political philosopher Jean Bodin in 1580: 'It is certain that [they] have a profound knowledge of all things. No theologian can interpret the Holy Scriptures better than they can: no lawyer has a more detailed knowledge of testaments, contracts and actions; no physician or philosopher can better understand the composition of the human body, and the virtues of the heavens, the stars, birds and fishes, trees and herbs, metals and stones.'

PRINCE OF DEMONS

The Devil himself, chief foe of both God and humans, is both the commanding demon and ruler of the underworld. In his incarnation as the prince of evil and arch tempter he is also known as Satan. He is thought to work his evil by laying claim to human souls, operating through the agency of demons, witches and the like. If bad luck befalls, could it therefore be the Devil's work?

According to legend, the Devil came into being when the archangel Lucifer ('light-bearer') attempted to rival God but failed in his mission and was cast out of heaven, a fallen angel. In the Bible, Lucifer is identified with Satan, the ruler of the underworld and God's arch enemy.

While some demonologists believe that Satan exercises his evil 'on licence' from God, testing

The Devil can take many forms and disguises, including a goat, a black dog and a wolf. In AD 447 he was described by theologians as 'a large black monstrous apparition with horns on his head, cloven hoofs ... an immense phallus and a sulphurous smell.'

humans in their faith, others think that he is God's rival, with his own autonomous powers. Through the centuries, human attitudes to the Devil have ranged from terror and contempt to worship. What is certain is that hundreds of superstitious practices, from baptism and hanging up a horseshoe to sowing parsley seeds on Good Friday (the only day when the soil is relieved of Satan's power), have been devised to keep the Devil at bay.

DEVILISH EXPRESSIONS

The Devil's powers of evil have led his name to be used in many ways:

DEVIL'S BONES	Dice made of bones; playing with them is a sure route to ruin.
TALK OF THE DEVIL	Said when someone mentioned in conversation makes an unexpected appearance.
GO TO THE DEVIL	Be ruined.
DEVIL-MAY-CARE	Reckless but cheerful.
DEVIL'S ADVOCATE	Someone prepared to take an unpopular view.
DEVIL'S DAUGHTER	A shrew.
THE DEVIL TAKE THE HINDMOST	Being selfish in competition.
THE DEVIL TO PAY	The certainty of trouble in store.

THE LITTLE PEOPLE

So strong was the belief in fairies in times past that parents would even kill a deformed or sick baby, imagining it to be a 'changeling' left by bad fairies.

Your luck will be in if a good fairy comes your way – but woe betide you if you are set upon by a bogie, goblin, bug-a-boo or some other evil fairy incarnation. And it's not just humans that fairies can affect. Cattle are said to be particularly susceptible to their powers.

Fairies are believed to live in an underground realm, with exits and entrances hidden in caves and hillsides. Some say they are the spirits of the dead, others that they are country deities and yet others that they are fallen angels. In medieval times it was a common belief that fairies not only spied on humans but could even interbreed with them. Even talking about fairies was, at that time, thought to be a sure way of bringing bad luck.

Good fairies are helpful to humans. They toil on the land and may even work magic by transforming rubbish into gold and jewels. In the home, brownies and other hobgoblins labour unseen, doing chores around the house. But they can turn malign if offended, contaminating food and drink.

A fairy ring, caused in fact by the growth of fungi in the grass, is said to be the place where fairies dance at midnight. Any human who chanced to fall asleep in the middle of a fairy ring would, it is said, fall into their clutches.

NEW PARENTS BEWARE: THE WORST MISCHIEF THAT A BAD FAIRY CAN DO IS TO SNATCH A BABY FROM ITS CRADLE. ONE NURSERY HOBGOBLIN, NAMED RAWHEAD-AND-BLOODY-BONES (WHICH HAD BLOOD RUNNING DOWN ITS FACE), WAS BELIEVED TO LIVE IN A CUPBOARD UNDER THE STAIRS, WHERE IT SAT ON A PILE OF THE BONES OF CHILDREN WHO HAD TOLD LIES OR SAID BAD WORDS. BAD FAIRIES CAN ALSO TAINT THE MILK OF CATTLE, MAKING IT CURDLE OR TURN TO BLOOD, WHILE THE LEGENDARY BAOBHAN SITH OF THE SCOTTISH HIGHLANDS, WHO LOOK LIKE BEAUTIFUL WOMEN, ARE IN FACT THIRSTY VAMPIRES IN SEARCH OF BLOOD.

WITCH POWER

From raising storms to poisoning people in body and mind, all manner of ill fortune is believed to be caused by witches. So evil are they said to be that, over the centuries, witch hunts have been commonplace.

The witch who casts her spell on you can, by common consent, make you mad, give you uncontrollable headaches, set your house on fire, ruin your friendships or even make you impotent. Being possessed by a witch will make you the perpetrator of all manner of foul deeds. The exceptions are the white witches who are thought to use their magical powers solely to do good deeds such as healing the sick, though historically this has afforded them no safety from persecution.

Why are they women? Because, say demonologists, women are more talkative than men, more ready to share their secrets, more impressionable and even more prone to hallucinations. From medieval times witches were thought to take the form described in this graphic account by Samuel Harsnett, who wrote a study of fiendish characters in 1599: '… an old weather-beaten crone, having the chin and her knees meeting for age, walking like a bow, leaning on a staff; hollow-eyed, untoothed, furrowed on her face, having her limbs trembling with the palsy, going mumbling in the streets …'

To work their evil, witches are said to meet annually at midnight on the Witches' Sabbath. As well as Halloween, Candlemas (2 February) was believed to be a common date for such evil get-togethers.

FAMILIAR TROUBLE

To carry out evil deeds on their behalf, witches were long thought to make use of familiars. These 'imps' traditionally took the form of animals, especially cats, but also toads, hares and dogs, and would often ride with the witch on her broomstick.

'… To consult, covenant with, entertain, employ, feed or reward any evil and wicked spirit' was enshrined as a crime in the English Witchcraft Act of 1604. Cats were the creatures most commonly invested with these powers, and so firmly was this idea entrenched that the burning of cats as 'devils' became routine. Black cats were most usually implicated. Some said that just one white hair rendered a feline incapable of performing magic of any kind.

Many of the superstitions associated with animals relate to their roles as familiars. Though it's generally thought lucky to be given a black cat it's said that the Devil will get you if you drown a cat. Killing toads is a long-held country way of protecting animals and humans from the ill effects of storms, while it is said that only a silver bullet will kill a hare.

Familiars have also been thought to take on human form. In the Lancashire witch trials of 1633, one of the accused, Margaret Johnson, confessed to consorting with Mamilion, a good-looking, well-dressed man.

WORD CHARMS

Sometimes, words will do. This is the belief behind spoken charms intended to dispel evil and cure disease. In witchcraft, charms are particularly associated with the casting of spells.

Although now associated with stage magic, in the Middle Ages it was customary to repeat the word ABRACADABRA. The earliest instructions for its use come from a poem on medicine by Quintus Serenus Sammonicus, a doctor and gnostic who accompanied the Roman Emperor Severus on an expedition to Britain in AD 208. For the charm to have maximum effect it must be written in the triangular form shown and hung around the patient's neck, in the belief that as the word got shorter, so would the malady.

ABRACADABRA
ABRACADABR
ABRACADAB
ABRACADA
ABRACAD
ABRACA
ABRAC
ABRA
ABR
AB
A

To dispel the power of witches – who increased the potency of their herbs and potions with habitual charm recitations – word-based antidotes were common and often invoked the name of the Saviour or the saints. The Church took a poor view of this and by the 17th century anyone found guilty of using such a charm could be found guilty of heresy and condemned to death by burning.

A CHARM WAND IS A GLASS WAND WITH A CURVED HANDLE LIKE A WALKING STICK, INTO WHICH ARE POURED HUNDREDS OF SMALL COLOURED SEEDS. THE LOGIC WAS THAT ANY INTRUDING WITCH OR DEMON WOULD BE TEMPTED TO COUNT THE SEEDS AND SO BE DISTRACTED (BY THE DIFFICULTY OF DOING SO IN DARKNESS) FROM ANY EVIL DEEDS. WIPING THE OUTSIDE OF THE WAND EACH MORNING WOULD RID IT OF ANY EVIL IT HAD ATTRACTED OVERNIGHT.

Lessons for Life

Having a long and happy, healthy and fulfilled life may have much to do with love and luck – and also, of course, the way we choose to behave.

Since human families first settled down together, risks and uncertainties have been smoothed out by society's rules. And it is these rules which, though now much changed in detail, form much of our modern legacy of law and morality, manners and behaviour. Religion – and especially the teachings of the Bible – has also been a dominant force in setting the standards of good and evil, and of behaviour in general, from 'love thy neighbour' to 'the love of money is the root of all evil'.

Such are life's pressures and pleasures, difficulties and desires that the wisdom of every age has been brought to bear on these subjects. Though today we may seek the help of psychiatrists, financial advisers and doctors to help maximize our talents and solve our problems, previous generations would have turned to their grand-parents, parents or the wise 'elders' of society. Much of their most valuable wisdom has been bequeathed to us, however, in proverbs, writings and sayings, as well as in books addressing everything from table manners to the way to conduct polite conversation.

When old advice meets new, modern science and medicine very often prove that granny was right after all, whether she was extolling the beneficial effects of a brisk walk or the need for a good night's sleep. However, we can all be grateful for the advances in health care that mean we no longer have to suffer untreatable pain. No more need for burnt mouse droppings to soothe the toothache!

Be Happy

Despite – or maybe because of – the riches we enjoy, contentment can remain elusive for, as one old proverb advises, 'all happiness is in the mind'. Nor are we doing anything new in seeking it out. Since ancient times people have been seeking the formula for fulfilment.

THE PATHS TO HAPPINESS

The routes to happiness are many and various, but the experts agree that there are many ways to achieve it, from good relationships with others to the sense of achievement we get from creating something or being a winner.

Does happiness come with the territory? People who live in Denmark, Iceland, Sweden, the Netherlands and Australia regularly rate themselves as being happiest with life. Work, not health or wealth, may be one of the keys to happiness. By asking a group of women to rate, on a scale of one to six, the episodes in their day, ranging from socializing with friends to commuting, a team at Princeton discovered that the most happiness came from having sex, relaxing with friends and having lunch with colleagues. Following these were watching TV alone and shopping.

The British zoologist and anthropologist Desmond Morris endorses some of these conclusions in his 'sources of elation',

---

AND CAN BEING MISERABLE MAKE YOU HAPPY? WORLDWIDE, THERE ARE PEOPLE (MORE OFTEN MEN THAN WOMEN) DUBBED 'QUERULOUS PARANOIDS' WHO ARE SO OBSESSED WITH THE FACT THAT THEY ARE VICTIMS OF INJUSTICE THAT FOR THEM MOANING AND GROANING BECOMES A WAY OF LIFE. THEIR GREATEST PLEASURE COMES FROM SUCH ACTIVITIES AS WRITING VOLUMINOUS LETTERS OF COMPLAINT IN BRIGHTLY COLOURED INKS.

which, as well as sex, include becoming a parent; co-operative behaviour (the pleasure of teamwork); the cerebral happiness of completing an intellectual task; the spiritual uplift of religious faith; the physical sensations of rhythmic movement such as dancing; and the happiness that comes from taking risks – the adrenalin (epinephrine) rush of anything from gambling to mountaineering. The 19th-century American agnostic, orator and lawyer Robert Ingersoll declared his creed to be:

Happiness is the only good.
The place to be happy is here.
The time to be happy is now.
The way to be happy is to make others so.

LAUGH IT OFF

As the old rhyme goes: 'Laugh and the world laughs with you. Cry and you cry alone.' Laughing is good for you, even though it can be hard to muster even a smile when life takes a turn for the worse.

Laughter does you good because, like exercise, it releases mood-lifting endorphins, which are also the body's natural painkillers. Also, it's been estimated that if you laugh for 20 seconds you breathe in as much extra oxygen (a known stress reliever) as you would get in three minutes of aerobic exercise. And it's almost impossible to stay tensed up while you're laughing.

Even without actually laughing, the part of your brain that controls happy emotions can stimulate your immune system to work harder, helping to stave off infections of all kinds, and possibly even cancer. One study reported in 2003 showed that for people over 50, thinking positively added an average of 7½ years to their lifespan.

Cracking up? 'Laughter is an instant vacation,' said comedian Bob Hope, when aged 96. He lived to 100. Long before, Lord Byron declared, 'Always laugh when you can. It is cheap medicine.'

The effectiveness of the joke, and of the laughter it provokes, lies in the way that humour allows us to offload our dangerous, aggressive and hostile instincts in a manner that is socially acceptable. For professional comedians, however, humour may be less beneficial. Many of them confess to feelings of deep depression at times when they are off stage.

HALF FULL?

For the optimist the glass is half full. For the pessimist it's half empty. As with laughter, a positive outlook on life is, literally, good for your health.

In a recent study, a group of heart attack survivors were each given a portable electrocardiogram machine to monitor their hearts in everyday situations. What emerged was that as soon as they experienced negative emotions their hearts began functioning less well, while positive emotions made their hearts beat better. With mental training, many of the patients learned to consciously 'up' their optimism and so improve their heartbeats.

Norman Vincent Peale, who died in 1993 aged 95, was the controversial author (widely pilloried for his New Age beliefs) of *The Power of Positive Thinking*. Written in 1952, it sold more than 20 million copies in 41 languages and became the model for a flood of self-help books.

When you're feeling positive, you may feel as if you're on 'cloud nine'. In one early classification of clouds of 1896, published in the abridged version of the International Cloud Atlas, *ten types were identified. Number nine was the white, fluffy, soft-looking cumulonimbus that has come to be associated with feelings of well-being.*

DOING GOOD

Good deeds do you good – that's a fact. It has long been known that virtue is its own reward, and we can all be cheered by the proverbial sentiment that what matters is not how long but how well we live.

Though the concept of 'loving your neighbour as yourself' is a tenet of the Biblical commandments, it has only recently been scientifically proved that kindness really can improve your health. Helping a neighbour just once a year can add to your life expectancy, even if it's as small a thing such as offering a lift or sharing a recipe.

Good works are charitable acts, but beware of becoming a 'do-gooder' – someone whose good deeds are unwelcome or, worse, who is self-righteous.

The 19th-century novelist Charles Kingsley personified good in his 1863 moral fantasy *The Water-Babies: A Fairy Tale for a Land-Baby* in the difference between the lovely Mrs Do-as-you-would-be-done-by and her fearsome sister Mrs Be-done-by-as-you-did. To Tom, the chimney sweep, the former had: 'The sweetest, kindest, tenderest, funniest, merriest face they ever saw, or want to see … she was a very tall woman, as tall as her sister: but instead of being gnarly and horny, and scaly, and prickly, like her, she was the most nice, soft, fat, smooth, pussy, cuddly, delicious creature who ever nursed a baby.'

Most modern educated women would heartily disagree with the sentiments expressed in the first line, though not the overall intention, of Kingsley's poem 'Farewell to C.E.G.':

Be good sweet maid, and let who can be clever;
Do lovely things, not dream them, all day long;
And so make Life, and Death, and that For Ever
One grand sweet song.

NO PLAY …

… and all work makes both Jack and Jill dull children. One effective route to a more satisfying, if not a happier, life is to get work and play in balance, though given the pressures of modern business life this is often easier said than done.

Getting the balance right, so as to be consistent with your true self or 'daimon', was the aim of the ancient Greeks. Your daimon represents the sense of excellence for which you strive, and which gives meaning and direction to your life. Modern psychologists believe that happiness is a skill that can be learned, and that being able to have fun is an important element of the whole.

Young animals such as lion cubs use play to learn the essentials of actions such as hunting down prey. For human children, play teaches co-ordination skills but in addition, if it is well directed, it fosters the development of thought, the channelling of aggression, communication, creativity and individual independence. Physical play also helps to keep children fit and control their weight.

'PLAY UP AND PLAY THE GAME' WAS A MOTTO OF COURAGE AND
GOOD SPORTSMANSHIP PENNED BY THE POET SIR HENRY NEWBOLT
(1862–1938) DURING WORLD WAR I IN HIS POEM 'VITAÏ LAMPADA',
IMPLYING THAT WAR SHOULD BE FOUGHT IN THE SAME SPIRIT AS
SPORTS. IT WAS WELL MEANT AND RECEIVED AT THE TIME, BUT
NEWBOLT LATER CAME TO DISLIKE ITS JINGOISTIC THEME INTENSELY.

Though the Egyptians competed in athletics, and played games
involving kicking leather balls stuffed with straw and hitting
balls with sticks, it was the Greeks who first formalized sport.
Of the various games that took place at sacred sites the most
important were the Olympic Games, held every four years
at Olympia in honour of Zeus, father of the gods. The first
recorded sporting victory, in 776 BC, was by a cook, Coroebus
of Elis, in the track race called the *stadion*.

YOU'RE AS OLD AS YOU FEEL

**Whatever the genetic hand you've been dealt, and despite
the fact that time will eventually take its toll, there are many
ways to stave off the ageing process. And there are countless
examples, past and present, to prove that it can be done.**

It's a medical fact that our biological and chronological ages
don't necessarily match up. As well as the luck of
the dice – long-lived parents are a great help – it is
also how you live that makes the difference. Of all
the things you can do to lower your biological age,
among the most advantageous are to live within
your means, visit friends at times of stress, and
(because gum disease can age your arteries), brush
and floss your teeth daily.

*Renowned for their
longevity, the people
of the Japanese island
of Okinawa favour
a diet rich in grains,
vegetables and fish,
with little meat,
poultry or eggs.*

Regular aerobic exercise is another key
ingredient. The secret? Exercise not only releases

'feel-good' chemicals called endorphins into the bloodstream but physical activity helps prevent thickening of the arteries (a well-known cause of high blood pressure) and may even remove potentially cancerous cells from the body. Add to that a diet rich in antioxidants (see p 180) and you have a good chance of keeping the fountain of youth from drying up.

LITTLE THINGS MEAN A LOT

It really is the small things in life that can make all the difference – the kind word, the modest indulgence, the gift of flowers. In health, too, regular treats can be good for you, and we should all be careful to read the small print.

Many small things can build up to good advantage. When tackling large tasks, it is good advice to get through them by setting many achievable intermediate goals. This can apply to anything from running a marathon to painting a room. Even with the smallest things it is worth paying attention to detail. In the words of Dale Carnegie, author of *How to Win Friends and Influence People*: 'Don't be afraid to give your best to what seemingly are small jobs. Every time you conquer one it makes you feel stronger ...'

'A nice cup of tea' is the age-old British remedy when things are going wrong, often accompanied by a biscuit. It was this tradition that led self-confessed 'biscuit freak' Stuart Payne to name his popular biscuit-review website nicecupofteaandasitdown.com – it receives over 50,000 hits a week.

The expression 'small is beautiful' was made popular by the economic theorist and author E.F. Schumacher in his 1973 book of the same name, subtitled *Economics as if People Mattered*. He proposed the idea of 'smallness within bigness': that is, for a large organization to work it must behave like a group of related small organizations.

SMALL MERCIES
Proverbial reasons why small things are to be valued:

- Small gifts make friends, great ones make enemies.
- Every little helps.
- The best things come in small packages.
- Small rain lays great dust.
- A short prayer penetrates heaven.
- A little pot is soon hot.
- Little and often fills a purse.
- Many drops make a shower.
- Little sticks kindle a fire, great ones put it out.

For Your Health

Once people called on the mercy of the gods to protect themselves from illness and to effect cures – a stark contrast to today's wealth of medical knowledge and range of treatments. Yet while we are ever more able to take care of our own health, many old-fashioned health 'saws' and remedies are still remarkably effective.

A LITTLE OF WHAT YOU FANCY

… does you good, goes the old saying. When it comes to healthy eating 'a little of a lot' is a good way to keep your appetite stimulated and your weight under control.

Variety can be beneficial for the mind, too, as the rhetorician Quintillian said: 'Our minds are like our stomachs; they are whetted by the change of their food, variety supplies both with fresh appetite.'

Moderation, and the avoidance of 'indulgence which presents a greater pleasure or a greater pain', was the ideal of the Greek philosopher, Epicurus of Samos, although the word 'epicurean' has come to be most often associated with the attitude of 'eat, drink and be merry'. Today, moderation is thought by the health professionals to be particularly helpful with weight control. Eating a little of what you like at frequent intervals during the day helps the stomach shrink (and therefore expect less food) and also helps to keep blood sugar levels steady.

Treats are good for you too! Plain chocolate boosts the levels of protective antioxidants in the blood, helping to keep arteries damage-free. (Without antioxidants tissues are damaged by

FOR A FIT BRAIN, DRINK A GLASS OF WINE A DAY. SO SAY RESEARCHERS ANALYSING THE RESULTS OF A TEN-YEAR STUDY OF 12,000 AMERICAN WOMEN. RED WINE IS BEST, BUT BEER AND SPIRITS CAN ALSO HELP TO STAVE OFF MENTAL IMPAIRMENT.

a kind of 'rusting' process caused by the release of oxygen from the tissues, a natural result of metabolism.) Additional benefits of adding dark chocolate to your diet are the production of the chemicals serotonin and dopamine, both of which have been proved to lift your mood.

NO PAIN, NO GAIN

The maxim coined to inspire the diligent doesn't seem much help when you're in agony from injury or headache. But pain is a necessary evil as it's an early warning system – without it we would suffer life-threatening or fatal injuries to our bodies without ever feeling a thing.

Is it worth it? Ovid, the Roman poet, thought so when he wrote: 'Endure and persist; this pain will turn to your good.'

Pain happens when receptors in the body tissues are triggered by some kind of damage. The messages they generate travel to the brain where they are perceived either as coming from a specific body part or as a general ache. Pain messages can be fast or slow, depending on the type of nerve fibres carrying the information. So when you stub your toe a short, sharp pain is usually followed by a duller, longer-lasting ache.

Because of the way nerve fibres are arranged, you don't always feel the pain where the problem is. Such 'pain referral' explains why you may feel a pain in your arm during a heart attack or the pain of an arthritic hip in your knee. Even more distressing is pain in a 'phantom limb' – a common occurrence following amputation.

THE HEALING TOUCH

From the moment babies first feel their mothers' touch, this most intimate of senses is the one we need to imbue us with feelings of safety and reassurance. Touch can heal our ills, whether it comes from another person or when we stroke a pet.

The physicians of ancient Greece were skilled masseurs, specializing in the treatment of stiff and painful joints. Writing in the 5th century BC Hippocrates, the father of medicine, declared that: 'The way to health is to have a scented bath and an oiled massage each day.' By 1895 doctors such as the American R.V. Pierce had correctly reached the conclusion that with massage '… the muscles are given elasticity and tone' and that from the skin 'innumerable dead epithelial cells, together with other impurities, are rolled off …'

In friendship, and more intimate partnerships, the hug is not only a signal of welcome, recognition and forgiveness but also an aid to health. And studies on couples have shown that when a man caresses a woman in a non-sexual way it can lower her blood pressure as much as a dose of prescription drugs. This works because stroking stimulates the brain to produce the hormone oxytocin, the calming substance that is also essential for a nursing mother to 'let down' her milk.

IT'S TRUE. ANIMAL LOVERS LIVE HEALTHIER LIVES BECAUSE STROKING A CAT OR DOG HELPS LOWER THE BLOOD PRESSURE. PETS ARE NOW REGULARLY BROUGHT INTO HOSPITALS FOR THE BENEFIT OF PATIENTS IN LONG-TERM CARE. THE EVIDENCE IS THAT PET CONTACT CAN DRAMATICALLY LIFT FEELINGS OF DEPRESSION.

YOU ARE WHAT YOU EAT

And drink. In the most literal sense, this is certainly true, as the old children's rhyme says: 'It's a very strange thing, as strange as can be – Whatever Miss T. eats turns into Miss T.'

It is a fact of life that the proteins, carbohydrates and fats in food are converted, after being digested, into the body's physical constituents. Proteins are the body builders, also used for general repairs

WRITING IN *HOW TO ENJOY HEALTH* IN THE LATE
1920S, DR CLAUDE LILLINGSTON ADVOCATED AN
'INTELLIGENTLY OMNIVOROUS' DIET FOR ADULT FIT-
NESS AND, FOR ALL CHILDREN, THE BANNING OF 'THE
EXCLUSIVE WHITE-BREAD-MARGARINE-TEA-SUGAR DIET'
AND THE INCLUSION OF FRESH FRUIT AND VEGETABLES.

of cells. Fats are burned for energy but are also vital for maintenance and, stored under the skin, give us valuable insulation from the cold. Carbohydrates also supply energy and are vital to the minute-by-minute workings, or metabolism, of every body cell.

The better the lifestyle of the cow, the better the beef. That is the conclusion of research into Scotland's Aberdeen Angus cattle. Those fed only on grass, not fattened on maize, have much higher levels of 'good' polyunsaturated fats.

But there is more to food than this. A quality diet, as free as possible from additives and packed with vitamins and minerals, improves the quality of life by boosting our immune systems, and by helping to protect us from diseases and allergies. A 'lean' diet, not excessive in calories, will also help keep the weight in check.

THE FEVERED BROW

Thanks to immunizations and antibiotics, we know today that all but the worst infections can be overcome with medical help. This is a far cry from the days when the fevers they triggered were often the dread preamble to death.

Fever – technically a body temperature raised above 37°C (99°F), measured in the mouth – is the

To cure a fever it was common practice to try to transfer it to an inanimate object. Often a handful of salt or an egg were buried in the ground for that purpose. Another remedy was for the patient to wear two 'under-linen garments' and for a relative or friend to tear a piece off the cloth nearest the skin each day until the sufferer recovered (or died) or the garment was completely destroyed.

body's natural reaction to infection and occurs when, as a result of white blood cells attacking infective agents such as bacteria and viruses, proteins called pyrogens are released into the blood and bring about a change in the temperature-controlling mechanism in the brain. In past times it was often called ague.

In the days when killer diseases such as typhoid, typhus, scarlet fever – and of course smallpox – were rife, seeing a patient through a fever was all-important. Doctors recognized four distinct fever stages: the forming stage; the cold stage; the hot stage; and the sweating or declining stage.

Each needed to be carefully managed. The outlook for victims was deemed to be good if they showed 'a natural and soft state of the skin, eruptions on the surface, a natural expression of the countenance, moist tongue, free action of the kidneys, and regular sleep.'

THAT THE ASPEN OR POPLAR TREE SHAKES IN THE WIND IS THE ORIGIN OF ITS USE AS A CURE FOR FEVERS. ONE COUNTRY REMEDY WAS RECORDED IN LINCOLNSHIRE WHEN A GIRL WITH A FEVER PINNED A LOCK OF HAIR TO THE TREE AND SAID: 'ASPEN-TREE, ASPEN-TREE, I PRITHEE TO SHAKE AND SHIVER INSTEAD OF ME.' BY ALL ACCOUNTS SHE RECOVERED.

WHAT A HEADACHE

'There is no ill to which flesh is heir that is the source of a greater discomfort to the human race than headache,' wrote Dr R.V. Pierce in his 1895 *People's Common Sense Medical Adviser*. 'The farmer, housewife, banker, merchant and laborer,' he continued, 'seem to be equally prone to ... this most unpleasant affliction.'

Today his opinion is confirmed and backed up by the statistic that the most common form of the problem is the tension headache, whose main symptom is a constricting band-like pain around the temples, often seeming to originate from the nape of the neck. Stress and anxiety are its major causes, as are noise, dehydration and illnesses such as colds and flu.

Less common, but much more unpleasant – since it is usually associated with nausea and aversion to bright light – is the migraine headache, known to have been suffered by Julius Caesar, St Paul, Immanuel Kant and Sigmund Freud. The Roman physician Aretaeus of Cappadocia, writing in the 2nd century AD, vividly described migraine, which he called 'heterocrania': '... in certain cases the whole head is pained ... It occasions unseemly and dreadful symptoms ... nausea;

RELIEVING THE PAIN
Some of the more bizarre folk remedies for headaches include:

- Drive a nail through a skull found in a graveyard, it will take on the pain for you.
- Drink cowslip cordial or eat the leaves of feverfew or wild lettuce.
- Tie a piece of hangman's rope around your head.
- Tie round your head a piece of a sheet that has previously wrapped a corpse.
- Get someone to measure the circumference of your skull with a piece of red yarn.
- To prevent one, wear the cast skin of an adder inside your hat.

vomiting of bilious matters ... there is much torpor, heaviness of the head ... flashes of purple or black colours before the sight, or all mixed together, so as to exhibit the appearance of a rainbow expanded in the heavens.'

A PAIN IN THE MOUTH

Even worse than a headache, though now, thanks to modern preventive dentistry, easier to cure for good, is toothache. Before the advent of anaesthetics, the treatment was just as painful as the problem, though strong alcoholic drinks were administered to help ease the agony.

Treating toothache goes back to the earliest civilizations. The first recorded dentist was an Egyptian sage named Hesy-Re in the 3rd millennium BC. Until dentistry became a respected profession, tooth-pulling – the easiest cure – was done by anyone, from a barber to a blacksmith, who felt themselves capable of ensuring a successful outcome. Cavity plugs made from resin and coral were used by the Egyptians, but 'drilling and filling' became routine only with the advent of amalgam in the 1800s.

Such was the pain of toothache that sufferers would ask for divine intervention. One typical request of 1696 included the words: 'Jesu Christ for Mary's sake, Take away this Tooth-Ach[e].' The words were written three times on separate pieces of paper, then burnt in the fire in succession.

The ancients had many cures for toothache, including the application of burnt mouse droppings or olive oil in which earthworms had been boiled. Oil of cloves is a long-used remedy. Its pungent taste is nothing compared with the sensation these 19th-century remedies for 'instant relief' must have produced: 'A drop of creosote, or a few drops of chloroform on cotton, applied to the tooth ... or a few grains of camphor moistened with turpentine.'

The moral, of course, is to prevent tooth decay in the first instance. Modern fluoride toothpastes now make this easy, but it's still wise to follow granny's advice and brush and floss night and morning, and to avoid sweets. And though granny may abhor it, chewing gum helps, too, by keeping saliva flowing, making the mouth an alkaline environment hostile to bacteria.

LEAVE WELL ALONE
Which means having the strength of mind to resist (as granny would have recommended) squeezing spots and picking at scabs. A little 'healthy neglect' can work wonders, as both doctors and gardeners will testify.

Even back pain, the scourge of the 21st century, usually gets better on its own. And with moderate activity (rather than staying in bed) a slipped disc can repair itself within six weeks.

Fiddling with spots and scabs – which are nature's ways of ridding the body of debris and healing its wounds – is obviously the easiest way of introducing infections. For other seemingly serious conditions, doing nothing can also be the best practice. The old adage that 'with treatment a cold lasts seven days, without it a cold lasts a week' still holds true, while doctors are ever more reluctant to remove children's adenoids, knowing that these naturally shrink after the age of four.

Procrastinate at your peril? Literature divides clearly into 'yes' and 'no' camps. For the poet

---

IT IS A FACT THAT MORE HOUSEPLANTS PERISH FROM OVER-WATERING THAN FROM ANY OTHER CAUSE. THOSE PARTICULARLY PRONE TO 'DEATH BY WATER' INCLUDE AFRICAN VIOLETS AND POINSETTIAS.

> *'While the grass grows, the horse starves' goes the old proverb.*

William Congreve the lesson was: 'Delay not till to-morrow to be wise;/To-morrow's sun to thee may never rise.' For the 18th-century American attorney Aaron Burr it was: 'Never do today what you can put off till tomorrow. Delay may give clearer light as to what is best to be done.'

IMPENDING DOOM?

Death comes to us all sooner or later, and countless super-stitions and tales relate to its prediction, particularly to family members. These range from objects seen in dreams to the sightings and behaviour of plants and animals.

Some sounds are regarded as particularly potent death omens. These include unexpected, unexplained crashes and bangs, often during the night (possibly linked to the fact that most deaths happen in the early hours of the morning, when body temperature is lowest) but also 'death-related' sounds such as those of coffins being made or of funeral processions. In Scotland people fear the 'dead-drap' – the hollow, leaden sound

COMMON DEATH OMENS

- If three people take part in making a bed someone will die in it within the year.
- A single bird tapping on the window.
- A bay tree that suddenly shrivels foretells the death of a king – or the outbreak of some deadly disease or pestilence.
- A butterfly seen flying at night.
- Hearing the call of the golden plover.
- Apple blossom appearing in autumn.
- One or two drops of blood fall from either side of the nose.
- A cat leaves the house when someone falls ill.

of water dripping from a height. The ominous clicking sound of the wood-burrowing (and destroying) death-watch beetle has long been regarded as a forewarning of impending death. A poem written by the satirist Jonathan Swift on one William Wood in 1725 observes:

But a kettle of scalding water injected.
Infallibly cures the timber affected;
The omen is broke, the danger is over;
The maggot will dye [sic], and the sick will recover.

Of Human Frailties

Try as we may, perfection in our lives is beyond our grasp, though some people undoubtedly come closer than others to this ideal. 'The world, the flesh and the Devil' are the classical triumvirate of evils we are taught to avoid, as well, of course, as the seven deadly sins.

ALL IS VANITY

Over-attentive self regard is behaviour generally considered to be undesirable. As a scene of empty, idle amusement and frivolity, Vanity Fair was one of the places described in John Bunyan's 1678 allegory *The Pilgrim's Progress*.

In advising women of their 'proper' qualities, *The Girl's Own Paper* of 1895 rails strongly against vanity, declaring that a woman would 'think herself dishonoured by charms that should make her an idol … always nestling in her shrine and waiting for the incense and homage of her adorers'. Yet however poor her attitude she would be spared the fate of the beautiful Greek youth Narcissus who, in punishment for spurning the love of the nymph Echo, fell in love with his own image, reflected in a pool of water, and pined to death.

In *Vanity Fair*, William Makepeace Thackeray's satire published in 1848, the weakness and folly of human nature is epitomized by his heroine Becky Sharp. For his title Thackeray borrowed the name of Bunyan's town, a place of all-year entertainment established by three evil forces, Beelzebub (the prince of Devils), Apollyon (king of Hell) and Legion (the numberless crowd). This place of temptation, like others such as the Valley of Humiliation and the Slough of Despond, was a key stage in the spiritual journey of Christian, the pilgrim in *The Pilgrim's Progress*.

A well-kept secret: the singer-songwriter Carly Simon has never revealed the subject of her 1973 hit 'You're So Vain', though speculation has leant towards the Rolling Stones' Mick Jagger.

BY VIGOROUS POLISHING OF THE SHINY MINERAL OBSIDIAN THE PEOPLE OF CATAL HÜYÜK IN MODERN TURKEY MADE THE FIRST KNOWN LOOKING GLASSES IN AROUND 6400 BC. THE SILVERED GLASS MIRRORS WE KNOW TODAY, AND WHICH ARE STILL THE FAVOURED ACCESSORIES OF THE VAIN, ORIGINATED IN VENICE DURING THE MIDDLE AGES.

THE DEADLY SINS

The notion of sin must, we presume, be as old as humankind, but it is brought into sharp focus by both moral teaching and religious belief. Though never actually defined in the Bible, Talmud or Qur'an, the seven deadly sins are regarded as vices it is wise to avoid – by both good believers and atheists alike.

The concept of the seven deadly sins, also known as the capital vices or cardinal sins – those that stand 'at the head'

THE SINS ENCOUNTERED

The souls in Dante's vision of Purgatory were forced to atone for their sins in specific and appropriate ways:

PRIDE .... By carrying a heavy weight tied around the neck, which prevented the wearer from standing up straight.

ENVY .... By having the eyes sewn shut and wearing clothes that made the soul indistinguishable from the ground.

WRATH .... By walking around in acrid smoke.

SLOTH .... By continual running.

AVARICE .... By lying face down on the ground.

GLUTTONY .... By abstaining from food or drink.

LUST .... By burning in a flaming river.

Competing for virtue: the Seven Deadly Sins board game is based on the same principles as snakes and ladders. Players start at Creation with the aim of reaching Nirvana, but are hampered on their way by spells cast on them by their opponents.

of other sins – have a history that certainly goes back to Pope Gregory I (St Gregory the Great), who died in AD 604, but they were described in their present form by St Thomas Aquinas in the 13th century. Ranked in order of severity, the sins are pride, envy, wrath, sloth, avarice, gluttony and lust.

That the seven deadly sins are so firmly embedded in our culture owes much to the *Divine Comedy* of Dante Alighieri, written in the early 14th century. The work describes an imaginary journey through the 'world of souls' of Hell, Purgatory and Heaven, and it is in Purgatory that the pilgrim is shown seven terraces, each devoted to the purging of one of the seven deadly sins.

THE BEAST WITHIN

It is said that a child born with one or more teeth already erupted will be possessed of an uncontrollable temper – or be doomed to suffer a violent death.

Anger, when properly handled, can, say the psychologists, be good for you, but allowed to get out of hand it can threaten our health – and even life itself. What matters is to be able to take responsibility for your anger and to allow yourself time to cool off.

On the bad side, both repeated expressions of hostility and repressed anger act to build up blood levels of homocysteine and cholesterol, substances both closely associated with heart disease. Unexpressed anger can also, it's thought, lead to depression, digestive problems, disturbed sleep and all kinds of ills. Angry people are, studies suggest, more likely to be prone to addictions, obesity, or both.

As well as learning to cool off before expressing anger – for instance by talking to someone, taking a walk or sitting quietly and breathing deeply until you decide on the best course of action – it is also possible to use your anger positively by channelling the energy it creates into a constructive activity, such as doing something for someone else.

TEMPER, TEMPER

From the plethora of writers' advice, a few choice nuggets:

- 'When anger rises, think of the consequences.' (Confucius)
- 'Anger in our mirth is like poison in a perfume.' (Joseph Addison)
- 'Watch against anger; neither speak nor act in it; for, like drunkenness, it makes a man a beast and throws people into desperate inconveniences.' (William Penn)
- 'When angry, count four; when very angry swear.' (Mark Twain)
- 'Anger is like/A full-hot horse, who being allowed his way,/Self-mettle tires him.' (William Shakespeare)

PASSING THE BUCK

It's so easy to put the blame on someone else! This was once done literally, using goats to take the rap for human failings, though President Harry S. Truman's desk famously bore the sign, mailed to him in October 1945, 'The buck stops here'.

Over history, many people have been scapegoated, often with disastrous consequences, from the Jews and gypsies who became victims of the Holocaust to the Colombian footballer Andrés Escobar, who was killed after scoring an own goal in the 1994 soccer World Cup.

The phrase 'pass the buck', meaning to evade blame or personal responsibility, or to shift it on to other shoulders, is credited to Mark Twain, who first used it in 1872. It refers to the game of poker and to the buckhorn-handled knife placed before a player to designate him as the next dealer. After each deal the knife was shifted to the next player around the table.

Much longer ago, the Hebrew Bible recounts the use of the scapegoat. Along with a bull, two goats were brought to a place of sacrifice. The high priest cast lots for which goat would be killed for a burnt offering and which – the scapegoat – would be saved. Placing his hands on the scapegoat's head the priest confessed the sins of the people of Israel. The creature was then led into the wilderness.

It was once common, following a death, for the living to undergo the practice of sin-eating. By consuming food that had been in contact with the corpse a designated 'sin eater' could take on the sins of the dead person, allowing them to rest in peace. Sin eaters were often poor people who undertook this duty in order to obtain a meal.

THE HABITS OF A LIFETIME

These work for good, when it comes to matters like manners and upright behaviour, but to our detriment when they turn into addictions that take over our lives and ruin those of others.

The Victorian compendium *Enquire Within* laid down a series of 20 good habits for 'a man of business', many of which still hold good. They included being 'strict in keeping engagements'; doing nothing 'carelessly or in a hurry'; leaving 'nothing undone that ought to be done, and which circumstances permit him to do'; and that he

---

TWELVE STEPS TO A SOLUTION

The 12-step programme has its origin in the formation of Alcoholics Anonymous (AA) in the 1930s and has been successful in helping many addicts. In précis, the steps are:

1. Admitting powerlessness over the addiction.
2. Believing that you can be restored.
3. Making a decision to turn your life over to a higher power.
4. Making a searching moral inventory of yourself.
5. Admitting to a higher power, and to other people, the nature of your wrongs.
6. Achieving a state of readiness for your character defects to be removed.
7. Humbly asking for your shortcomings to be removed.
8. Listing everyone you have harmed, and becoming willing to make amends to all.
9. Making those amends.
10. Continuing to make a personal inventory and admitting to wrongs.
11. Seeking to improve conscious contact with a higher power.
12. Carrying the message to other addicts, and practising its principles.

---

should be 'economical in his expenditure, always living within his income'. The advice ends by saying that 'success will attend his efforts' if all these are accomplished.

More than a century later, the evidence suggests that the stresses of life are among the triggers for the bad habits that end up as addictions. Most at risk, whether from alcohol, tobacco, drugs or gambling, are those who have an 'addictive personality', a condition now thought to have a strong genetic component.

VENGEANCE IS MINE

Women scorned: well-documented cases of revenge include women cutting off the sleeves of their unfaithful husbands' shirts and suits, crashing their cars and pouring away (or enjoying drinking) their finest wines.

Revenge, the dish 'best served cold' is the long-used way of getting even with your enemy, even if it means going to war, on the premise that 'if you can't get mad, get even'. Though proverbially sweet, revenge may not always have the lasting effect you desire.

The Bible, predictably, has plenty to say about revenge. But while the Old Testament concept was of 'an eye for an eye and a tooth for a tooth', the preaching of Jesus advocated turning the other cheek: 'Therefore if thine enemy hunger, feed him; if he thirst, give him drink; for in so doing thou shalt heap coals on his head.'

Francis Bacon, the English essayist, scholar and statesman had much to add in his essay 'Of Revenge', published in 1625, in which he wrote: 'Revenge is a kind of wild justice; which the more man's nature runs to, the more ought law to weed it out. For as for the first wrong, it doth but offend the law; but the revenge of that wrong, putteth the law out of office. Certainly, in taking revenge, a man is but even with his enemy; but in passing it over, he is superior; for it is a prince's part to pardon.'

He also wrote: '... Some, when they take revenge, are desirous the party should know whence it cometh. This is the more generous. For the delight seemeth to be not so much in doing the hurt as in making the party repent ...'

With Best Intent

Acting honestly, acquiring knowledge and striving for both freedom and justice are the ideals of good people everywhere. Though aware of our human failings, we nonetheless strive for both individual success and honour while hugely admiring the courage and heroism of the few.

IF AT FIRST …

Success is all a matter of perspective – and usually perseverance. For some it means money, power and adulation, for others the happiness that a fulfilling life can bring. In sport, the thrill of winning is key.

Perseverance – and for many skills and sports practice – are vital to success. In training the body and brain to perform in harmony, many athletes make use of so-called autogenic techniques. By repeating key phrases such as 'The target focuses my mind' to themselves, performers such as marksmen become able to find a balance between relaxation and arousal, which allows them to perform at their best.

IN JAPAN, UNDAUNTED PERSEVERANCE IN THE FACE OF DEFEAT, EVEN IF THIS INVOLVES PERSONAL HUMILIATION, IS DEEMED ONE OF THE HIGHEST PERSONAL QUALITIES, A FACT BORNE OUT IN MANY OF THEIR TV 'ENDURANCE' GAME SHOWS.

The 'inner game' is another popular method of mind-training in sport. Exponents describe activities in terms of Self 1, the person who tells us what to do and then how we should do it, and Self 2, the person who carries out the action. Self 1 is taught, by degrees, to be less judgmental and negative with regard to errors, while Self 2 is left free to become more spontaneous.

QUOTE ME
Much has been said, by many, about success:

* 'Man learns little from success, but much from failure.' (Arabic proverb)
* 'If you wish success in life, make perseverance your bosom friend, experience your wise counsellor, caution your elder brother and hope your guardian genius.' (Joseph Addison)
* 'In the lexicon of youth, which fate reserves/For a bright manhood, there is no such word /As – fail.' (Edward Bulwer-Lytton)
* 'Try not to become a man of success but rather to become a man of value.' (Albert Einstein)
* 'If you don't tell people about your success, they probably won't know about it.' (Donald Trump)

A LITTLE KNOWLEDGE

… is a dangerous thing, it's said. However, the proverb writers also tell us that 'Knowledge is power' and that 'Much learning makes men mad'. That said, learning something new every day is a great way of keeping the brain in trim.

The ability to learn is, indeed, one of the most powerful human attributes, our way of understanding – and assessing – the world and everything and everyone in it. As the 17th-century philosopher John Locke declared: 'Knowledge, which is the highest degree of the speculative faculties, consists in the perception of the truth of affirmative or negative propositions.' That it is useful was eloquently summed up by Shakespeare: 'Ignorance is the curse of God,/Knowledge the wing wherewith we fly to heaven.'

In the Bible, the tree from which Eve, then Adam, ate the forbidden fruit was 'the tree of the knowledge of good and evil' which was 'pleasing to the eye and desirable for the knowledge it could give'. By listening to the cunning serpent and succumbing to temptation 'the eyes of both of them were opened, and they knew that they were naked'.

Acquiring knowledge involves many different parts of the brain, and such aspects as language, spatial awareness and memory. But as well as the thousands of specific facts our brains store in a lifetime, what's most helpful in daily life is the accumulated wisdom that comes from experience – good and bad – and, even more crucially, the ability to see, and achieve in a practical way, the solutions to problems. Also important is being able to appreciate when you don't have enough knowledge, and seeking or asking for the help you need.

HONOUR BOUND

Honour can be a matter of noble behaviour or, as in Britain where an 'honours system' still exists, one of rank. In times past an affair of honour was a matter settled by a duel.

'Honour thy father and thy mother' is the fifth of the commandments given by God to Moses on Mount Sinai. In the Old Testament, The Book of Ecclesiastes, a text packed with advice, also demands of the godly that they act so as to 'leave not a stain in thine honour'.

In the New Testament Jesus, when his provenance was questioned by the inhabitants of Nazareth, his home town, declared: 'A prophet is not without honour, but in his own country, and among his own kin, and in his own house.'

In Britain, the title 'Honourable' is one given to the children of life peers, or to royal maids of honour (unmarried women attending a queen or princess). 'Right Honourable' is the title given to members of the Privy Council. In the USA, it is a courtesy title given to people holding high office, especially in the legal profession or in civic life.

According to an old Welsh proverb: 'Be honourable yourself if you wish to associate with honourable people.'

The granting of honours by the British monarch – on the recommendation of the government – is generally announced twice annually, at New Year and on the Queen's official birthday in June. The most common honour is that of OBE (Order of the British Empire). Among knighthoods the oldest honour is the Most Noble Order of the Garter. Originally, knights were those to whom the sovereign granted the right to bear arms.

DR JOHNSON'S HONOURS

In his Dictionary *of 1755 Samuel Johnson listed 13 meanings of 'honour':*

1. Dignity, high rank.
2. Reputation; fame.
3. The title of a man of rank.
4. Subject of praise.
5. Nobleness of mind; scorn of meanness; magnanimity.
6. Reverence; due veneration.
7. Chastity.
8. Dignity of mein [majesty].
9. Glory; boast.
10. Publick [*sic*] mark of respect.
11. Privileges of rank or birth.
12. Civilities paid.
13. Ornament; decoration.

TAKE COURAGE

In everyday life we often 'screw up our courage' or take the plunge, and are urged to have 'the courage of our convictions' but it is in times of danger, especially in battle, that courage is a virtue to be especially honoured.

That we should all aspire to be courageous is summed up by the exhortation of Theodore Roosevelt, US President from 1901 to 1909: 'You have got to have courage. I don't care how good a man is, if he is timid his value is limited. The timid will not amount to very much in this world. I want to see a good man ready to smite with the sword. I want to see him able to hold his own in an active life against the forces of evil.'

Military honours to recognize acts of courage exist worldwide. Among the oldest is the German honour, *Pour le Mérite*, more popularly known as the 'Blue Max', which dates back to 1740. The French have awarded the *Légion d'honneur* since 1802. David Lucas, then a midshipman but later a Rear Admiral, was the first recipient of the Victoria Cross, Britain's highest honour for military bravery. During the Crimean War a Russian shell landed on the deck of HMS *Hecla*. While his compatriots dived for cover, Lucas picked up the live shell with its burning fuse and tossed it overboard.

In America, the Medal of Honor was instigated during the Civil War, originally to 'promote efficiency of the Navy', by an Iowa senator, James W. Grimes, in 1861. The following year the equivalent medal for the army followed and was first awarded to Army Assistant Bernard J.D. Irwin, who had rescued 60 soldiers at Apache Pass, Arizona, on 13 February 1861.

JUSTICE FOR ALL

'The virtue by which we give to every man what is his due' was the definition of justice given in Dr Johnson's 1755 *Dictionary*, but it has been the aim of the law since ancient times. However, injustice has long been summed up in the proverbial statement, 'There is one law for the rich, and another for the poor.'

That our own judgment should be impartial and personal was neatly summed up by the American writer Henry James: 'Don't mind anything that anyone tells you about anyone else. Judge everyone and everything for yourself.'

The earliest known lawmaker and dispenser of justice was the Babylonian king Hammurabi, whose rule began around 1792 BC. His code imposed the death penalty for a wide range of crimes, and stated that a man held responsible for the death of his employer's son should sacrifice his own son in recompense. In the West, one of the earliest codes of justice was England's Magna Carta, sealed by King John in 1215. It stated that 'No freeman shall be taken … imprisoned … or in any other way destroyed … except by the lawful judgment of his peers, or by the law of the land.'

In Norman Britain juries were groups of people brought to court by virtue of their knowledge of the case in hand. This was based on an old German custom. William the Conqueror appointed England's first judges in the late 11th century.

The first juries of ancient Greece were chosen at random. The philosopher Socrates was found guilty of impiety and corruption of the young by the majority of a jury of 501; to carry out his death sentence he was required to drink hemlock.

Mind Your Manners

Manners and etiquette are not only social lubricants but a due acknowledgment of our respect for the thoughts and wishes of others. And while we may cheer at today's breakdown of the old barriers of class and money, and the complex rules of polite society, good manners remain a valuable asset.

Advocating good manners at all times, but especially at home, the 1950 Manners for Moderns bemoans the poor manners displayed between husband and wife, though 'no woman could bear a husband who kept leaping to his feet every time she carried a plate of bread and butter'. It concludes that: 'Good manners between married people are more a question of attitude than punctiliousness.'

WHY MANNERS MATTER

Since the days of medieval chivalry, polite society has demanded certain standards which have, for at least 500 years, been the subject of 'manners manuals' of all kinds. Though the rules are now more relaxed than ever, politeness is still the oil that reduces friction in all our personal contacts.

The Babees' Book, written in the 15th century and intended for pages and maids in waiting, instructed on the proprieties of doffing (removing) headwear in front of a lord and on practical matters such as washing the hands before meals. *De civitate morum puerilium (On the Civility of the Behaviour of Boys)*, a treatise of 1530 by the Dutch scholar Desiderius Erasmus, concentrated on good manners in school and at church.

By the 19th century, attention to etiquette had not only become extraordinarily complex, but was seen as a moral obligation. The Victorian manual *Enquire Within* lists dozens of rules including 'avoid falsehood', 'be sincere in your friendships' and 'beware of foppery and silly flirtation', and declares: 'How captivating is gentleness of manner derived from true humility, and how faint is every imitation!' *Etiquette*, subtitled *The Blue Book of Social Usage* and first published in 1922, became the American 'bible' of manners, and in 1946 its author founded the Emily Post Institute, whose purpose was 'to perpetuate the tradition of gracious living by making available the most recent information on etiquette …'

Also in the USA, Judith Martin – 'Miss Manners' – advises on 'Excruciatingly Correct Behaviour' in the *Washington Post* and other newspapers. Miss Manners is 'unfailingly polite' and 'believes that, if one always does the right thing, one does not have to read nasty little books about how to deal with guilt.'

THE PERFECT GENTLEMAN

Rules of behaviour are more or less the same today for men and women, particularly in the workplace. However, it was not always so. In the past a gentleman would be judged, by both women and his peers, by both his demeanour and his every action.

Among the traditional rules of etiquette are those that state that a man should stand when a lady enters the room, that he should remove his hat when entering a church and that he should open the door for his female companion. That a man should walk on the outside of the pavement is simply protective behaviour. In doing so he allows himself to be splashed by water or mud from passing traffic.

A gentleman's agreement is one made – and always kept – on a spoken promise and a handshake. There is no need for it to be written down.

As a host, a gentleman's role, says the American author Florence Howe Hall, 'is necessarily [as] a temporary

GENTLEMANLY BEHAVIOUR

Enquire Within *listed rules for a gentleman, all of them 'worthy of frequent meditation' and of high moral tone, including:*

- To be wise in his disputes
- To be a lamb in his home
- To be brave in battle and great in moral courage
- To be discreet in public
- To be a bard in his chair
- To be a teacher in his household

- To be conscientious in his actions
- To be happy in his life
- To be diligent in his calling
- To be just in his dealing
- To do whatever he doth as being done unto God, and not unto men.

ruler' – though even in 1887 she complained that 'the modern host is but a shadow of his former prototype', the onus of entertaining having passed to women. As a guest she warns against 'lingering leave taking … When a gentleman takes his leave' she continues, 'it suffices for him to make a decided bow to the lady of the house, with a slighter inclination to the other members of the family.'

LADYLIKE BEHAVIOUR

Previously denoting a woman of high rank, the word 'lady' also once meant, as Dr Johnson records, 'an illustrious or eminent woman'. While it no longer relies, every day, on unswerving deference, ladylike behaviour is still expected in polite society.

Even in the 1960s, girls sent to 'finishing schools' were taught such ladylike manners as never smoking or eating in the street, always wearing hat and gloves for church, never being without a handkerchief and never keeping a man waiting (but equally never making the first move or paying for dinner on a date). A girl was also taught that she need not feel guilty if, at the end of an evening, she rejected a man's advances and merely wished him goodnight.

The word 'lady' derives from an Old English word meaning 'bread kneader', indicating a woman's role in the household and family.

The complex business of visiting and the correct use of visiting cards was once of great concern to ladies. A well-educated woman would know that 'a lady does not put her address on her visiting card', and that friendly calls should be made in the morning but formal ones never before noon. 'When a mistress takes a house in a new locality,' said Mrs Beeton, 'it will be etiquette for her to wait until the older inhabitants of the neighbourhood call upon her; thus evincing a desire, on their part, to become acquainted with the newcomer.'

Until the 1930s, middle-class women would employ a lady's maid, who would be expected to be 'a good needlewoman' and 'able to renovate or alter any garment'. She would assist her mistress to dress and would also be expected 'to do some of the finer washing, such as lace, gloves or evening handkerchiefs'.

WHEN AT TABLE

It is common sense and courtesy, and often the best way to prevent accident and injury, to avoid eating from the knife or talking with your mouth full. The other cardinal rule of good table manners is not to draw attention to yourself. On formal occasions it is often easiest to wait and see what others do before launching into action.

Good manners of the old style dictate that a man should hold out the chair for the woman on his right, and that no one should start eating until everyone at the table has been served (unless the hostess declares otherwise). You should refrain from putting your elbows on the table, slouching or tipping the chair, and use your napkin delicately and never, Emily Post warns, like 'a washcloth. Blotting or patting the lips,' she goes on, 'is much more delicate.'

For knives and forks the general rule is to work from the outside in. The American custom of cutting meat then changing the fork from the left to the right hand is not incorrect (another of Emily Post's rulings) but, she says, makes eating complicated. The custom probably arose from the days when knives were expensive and the one family blade was passed around the table for each member to use in turn.

EATING ETIQUETTE

Even today it may save embarrassment to know the traditionally well-mannered way to eat certain foods:

- SOUP – tip the bowl and move the spoon away from you; sip from the side of the spoon.
- BREAD – break into moderate-sized pieces with the fingers and butter them individually before eating.
- ASPARAGUS – use a knife and fork, but cut off the points and eat with a fork only; fingers are for family occasions only.

- PEAS – use a fork.
- SALAD – use a knife and fork (especially when leaves are large and springy).
- CHEESE – small morsels should be placed with a knife on small morsels of bread and the two brought to the mouth with the thumb and finger.
- UNCOOKED CHERRIES, PLUMS AND UNHULLED STRAWBERRIES – eat with the fingers.

DRINKING AND OTHER PLEASURES

As well as choosing wines appropriate to the food, the well-mannered host will know how best to serve them. He will also offer appropriate cocktails or pre-dinner drinks and, after dinner, port, brandy or liqueurs. For those who still indulge, cigars may be smoked.

Cigars are traditionally offered at dinner once the ladies have left the room. Smoking is now becoming generally unacceptable, but the much admired wartime premier Winston Churchill was rarely seen without a cigar. He adopted the habit after reporting on the Cuban rebellion of 1895–6.

Though the convention of white wine with fish and red with meat no longer holds in every circumstance, it is still a helpful rule. A good guide for choosing wine is to think of it as an 'ingredient' of the dish, which would lead you to choose an acidic wine such as a Muscadet with fish in much the same way as you would squeeze lemon over it, and to choose a full-bodied red wine like a Merlot to accompany beef or game.

Chilled – but never over-chilled – is the rule for white wines, which are never decanted. Reds, with the exception of young Bordeaux, should be at room temperature. Claret, or any wine likely to contain sediment, should be decanted, as should sherry and port. Sherry was once commonly served with the soup course.

If you are unlucky enough to open a corked wine it will have the rotten smell of the chemical trichloroanisole (TCA). If you are in a restaurant, no sommelier worth his keep will refuse to exchange such a bottle. The conventional way to taste a wine to be served with food is to roll a little around the glass (warming the glass in your hand for red wine) before sampling first the aroma and then the taste.

SHAKE ON IT

The handshake is a signal of greeting and friendship, a remnant of the ancient pledge of honour and the even earlier sealing of a contract. To the Romans, who greeted each other with outstretched arms and open palms, it also signified an absence of weapons.

Writing simply as 'A Member of the Aristocracy', an author of 1913 maintained that 'The gentlemen who shake hands with great warmth and empressment are two distinct individuals; the one is cordial and large-hearted, and has a friendly grasp for everyone – a grasp indicative of kindliness, geniality, and good fellowship – the other wishes to ingratiate himself in certain quarters, and loses no opportunity of demonstratively shaking hands, but no one is deceived by this spurious imitation of the real thing.'

In place of the handshake, Maoris greet each other by rubbing noses, while Indians put their palms together, with fingers pointing upwards, in a graceful gesture known as namaste.

The old-fashioned rule when meeting people is that it is the woman who should always offer her hand to a man in a handshake, not the other way around, though she 'should not offer to shake hands with one not expectant of the honour'. For both men and women, the firm (but not super-grip) handshake is recommended today in preference to the 'wet fish' or 'boneless' type, especially in business situations. Politicians, when shaking hands with – and trying to elicit support from – members of the electorate, often place their left hand over the hand of the person they are meeting in a gesture of intimacy. It was once common for both men and women to accompany the handshake with a bow, especially to someone of higher social rank. This was made 'first by inclining the head' then bending from the shoulders or waist, depending on the degree of deference intended.

MAY I INTRODUCE …

The need for introductions arises in all manner of social and business occasions. Properly done an introduction can convey useful information and avoid embarrassing *faux pas*. At a very formal ball or reception, a butler or master of ceremonies will announce guests as they arrive.

'In all cases,' says 'A Member of the Aristocracy' in his 1913 book *Rules*, 'introductions … should not be indiscriminately made – that is to say, without a previous knowledge on the part of those making them as to whether the persons thus introduced will be likely to appreciate each other, or the reverse, or unless they have expressed a desire to become acquainted.' And the effects of getting it wrong? 'An undesired introduction, if made,' he avers, 'compels the one to whom it is most unwelcome, to treat the other with marked coldness …'

Such a situation is unlikely to arise today, but it is still helpful to know, through a carefully worded introduction, whether people are married or not, whether they are colleagues, members of the family or prefer to be known by a nickname. Where rank is concerned, the rule is to introduce a woman without a title to a titled woman, younger to older and so on.

REMEMBER THE NAME. IT'S VERY EASY TO FORGET THE NAMES OF PEOPLE TO WHOM YOU ARE INTRODUCED. ONE GOOD TRICK IS TO REPEAT THE NAME IN YOUR RESPONSE: 'HOW DO YOU DO, MARY BROWN,' OR SOMETHING SIMILAR. OR, IF YOU CAN, LINK A PERSON'S NAME OR APPEARANCE WITH A MEMORABLE OBJECT.

IN A WORD

Saying the right thing, and knowing how to write using correct punctuation and spelling, are traditional skills not always employed or even applauded today. In 1916 Bernard Shaw was able to make great play in *Pygmalion* of the fact that the way you spoke and what you said immediately informed others of your social standing.

Slips of the tongue are easy to make, but it is a mercy that politeness no longer necessitates avoiding saying 'Pardon' when you mean 'Excuse me' or 'I'm sorry I didn't hear that'. No

Among Emily Post's long list of 'taboo' phrases were 'an invite', 'the wife', 'mansion' (i.e. a big house'), 'boy' (when meaning a man over 21), 'lady friend' and 'lovely food'.

one would nowadays expect a man to refer to 'Mrs Jones' when he meant 'my wife'. Indeed, the jocular 'her indoors', adopted following the success of the character Arthur Daley in the British TV hit *Minder*, is even acceptable in some informal situations.

When addressing a married woman by letter the custom of using the form 'Mrs John Smith' is rapidly dying out. The mannerly thing to do is to ask her how she prefers to be addressed. The same is even more true of unmarried women, most of whom feel strongly for or against the use of 'Ms'.

WITH OR WITHOUT AN 'H'?

A Victorian 'memorandum' on the use of the letter H recommended the dropping of the initial H in the pronunciations of:

'ERB

'EIR

'ONESTY

'ONOUR

'OSPITAL

'OUR

'UMOUR

'UMBLE

'UMILITY

'In all other cases, the H is to be sounded when it begins a word.'

'Be careful' it guided, 'to sound the H slightly in such words as where, when, what, why – don't say were, wen, wat, wy.'

BAD BEHAVIOUR

Although it can be accidental, bad behaviour is more likely to be a deliberate insult in gesture or word. Taken too far, insults both written and spoken can land you in court.

A gesture alone can often be the most cutting of insults. Today the single raised finger is commonly used, particularly as a sign of road rage. In the 18th and 19th centuries 'thumbing the nose' was the favoured gesture. It was used as a device by Thackeray in *The Rose and the Ring* in 1854 and appears in one of the 'Phiz' illustrations of Charles Dickens's *Bleak House*, published the previous year.

The V-sign (famously reversed as a victory sign by Winston Churchill in World War II) is thought to have begun in 1415. On the eve of the Battle of Agincourt, the French threatened to chop off the first and second fingers – the 'bow' fingers – of the English archers. Next morning, the English extended their undamaged digits in mockery of their defeated opponents.

While slander is an oral insult, libel, which is written down, is an actionable one. The word originally meant a 'little book', and a plaintiff's written statement – because it also made a small volume – was also dubbed a libel in some courts.

Arguably the worst insult to receive is the 'cut' – when you are ignored or snubbed. The cut can be delivered as a blank but pointed stare into your face (the cut direct), a look to the heavens (the cut sublime), a deliberate look in the other direction (the cut indirect) or by stooping to adjust the shoe until you have passed by (the cut infernal).

UNACCUSTOMED AS I AM

Making speeches is an art that demands thought, preparation and practice in front of a mirror – or a critical home audience. If anecdotes and jokes are to be included then even more skill is required.

Successful speech makers will agree that there are some cardinal rules of performance. Decide what you want to say, always keeping the purpose of the speech in mind. Say it as briefly as possible (though not with undue haste). Unless witty ideas come naturally, don't try too hard to be funny. Don't rush it. Look and behave as if you are enjoying yourself.

The ancient Greeks set much store by speeches. In the words of the great orator Demosthenes: 'As a vessel is known by the sound, whether it be cracked or not, so men are proved by their speeches whether they be wise or foolish.'

George Robey, the music hall star famous in the early 20th century who was dubbed 'The Prime Minister of Mirth', recorded in his *After Dinner Stories* plenty of advice for the would-be raconteur, which is also helpful to the speech maker. 'One of the most objectionable species of story-teller,' he says, 'is the individual who thinks his stories are so humorous that he roars with laughter at the very thought of what he is going to recount.' Equally: 'In telling an anecdote … the pithier the story the more telling it becomes.'

WOMEN'S WEAR

Dress for women has never been less formal, but it is still embarrass-ing to arrive at a function over- or underdressed. Which is why it is always advisable to check in advance if you can, especially for a formal occasion. And there is always the weather to consider …

Simplest may often be best. Advising on the propriety of dress, an American etiquette manual of the 1890s maintains that while 'a woman of society does not make dress her chief object, she is ordinarily anxious it should be well chosen, harmonious, striking in refinement and in style, and above all not overdone … She eschews "loud" patterns, conspicuous sleeves and capes and hats …'

Dressing for the weather and temperature led women in rural Britain to favour, for day wear, chunky tweeds and knitwear. From the early 1900s working women worldwide took to the two-piece skirt suit or 'costume'. Trousers for women became popular leisure wear from the late 1920s but did not become widely acceptable as formal dress until the 1970s.

'In your clothes,' wrote the English statesman Sir George Savile in *The Lady's New Year's Gift, or Advice to a Daughter* in 1688, 'avoid too much gaudiness; do not value yourself upon an embroidered gown; and remember that a reasonable word, or an obliging look, will gain you more respect than all your fine trappings.'

EXCEPT WITH EVENING DRESS, GLOVES ARE NOW NECESSARY ONLY FOR WARMTH, BUT EVEN 50 YEARS AGO A WOMAN WOULD BE EXPECTED TO WEAR THEM FOR EVERY OCCASION, FROM LUNCHEON TO A THEATRE DATE. AND A LADY WOULD NEVER REMOVE HER GLOVE TO SHAKE HANDS.

WELL SUITED

Long gone are the days when a man would be expected to wear a frock coat to the office, but the modern trend of 'smart casual' can be even more confusing than conforming to set rules. It's vital, too, to know how to dress for both 'black tie' and 'white tie' occasions.

'Never wear brown in town' is the old mantra advising men on shoe colour, the implication being that black shoes are always *de rigueur* with a lounge suit, the standard business wear since the 1920s. White socks are also a social taboo. 'Don't cover yourself with chains, fobs, lodge emblems etc.' warns Emily Post, and 'don't wear plaid shirts and neckties. You will only make a bad impression on everyone you meet.'

Black tie means wearing a dinner jacket. The alternative is the tuxedo, introduced in the 1890s at the Tuxedo Club, northwest of New York, as a less formal warm weather alternative to the 'swallowtail' or full evening dress, or to 'white tie', consisting of tail coat and a white shirt with a butterfly collar. With both black and white tie, patent leather shoes are the accepted 'uniform'.

SINCERE THANKS

Saying thank you, even if merely in 'bread and butter' fashion, is a courtesy to one's hosts. Whether or not to tip – especially if the service has been below par – is entirely another matter.

A written note of thanks for a gift, or following a meal with friends, is polite, welcome, and a social 'must'. To a hostess it should, as one 1950s guide puts it 'add that little extra gesture of gratitude which to some extent repays the hostess for the trouble she has taken for her guests' comfort and entertainment'. It should also 'make some reference to a return of the hospitality in the near future'.

The expectations of a tip 'at your discretion' depends on where you live. In Britain 10 per cent is still the norm, but elsewhere is more likely to be 12½ or even 15 per cent. What takes the courage and firmness that many find hard to muster, when service has been poor, is to deduct a tip that has already been added to your bill.

In the days when long-distance travel by ship was the norm it would be customary for passengers to tip a long list of staff, including the bath steward, cabin steward, deck steward, dining-room steward, stewardess, bar steward and baggage steward. We should be grateful that it has never been necessary to tip airline staff!

The Best Relations

Maintaining good relationships with our families, friends and neighbours is a sure-fire way to underwrite a life of maximum quality and happiness. But you always need to be careful what you do and say, for granny's maxim that 'Sticks and stones will break my bones, but words will never hurt me' does not always hold true.

A MATTER OF LOYALTY

No man, it is said, can serve two masters. Whether to country or employer, family or football team, loyalty is the cement that helps bind people together as a nation, at work and at play. It is the real and metaphorical rats that leave the sinking ship.

The word 'loyalty' first came into use in English in the 15th century, to signify the ideal of constant devotion and the way in which society was organized. In medieval times, the landowner or tenant-in-chief was granted land by the monarch – to whom he gave his loyalty and devotion – as a reward for services rendered, which included providing soldiers to defend the realm. In turn, the tenant-in-chief let his land to knights, who swore to defend him loyally, and to serve the monarch as required. Farmers and other servants of the knights pledged loyalty to their masters, and so on down the line.

When, in time, the feudal order was overturned, and royal power either diluted or dispensed with altogether, loyalty became something that an individual could freely give, but it could also be subject to legal contract. The word 'loyalist' then became particularly associated, in the American War of Independence, with those who sided with the British, many of whom eventually settled in Canada.

On matters of employment and loyalty, the prolific American author Elbert Hubbard, editor of the magazine *The Philistine* (who incidentally met his end on the *Lusitania* when it sank in 1915), said: 'If you work for a man, in Heaven's name work for him. If he pays you wages, which supply you bread and butter, work for him; speak well of him; stand by him and stand by the institution he represents. If put to a pinch, an ounce of loyalty is worth a pound of cleverness ...'

THERE IS NOTHING MORE VALUABLE TO SHOPKEEPERS THAN LOYAL CUSTOMERS. IN THE 1960S, STORES BOOSTED LOYALTY BY GIVING AWAY BLUE CHIP, GREEN SHIELD AND OTHER TRADING STAMPS, WHICH WERE COLLECTED BY THE MILLION AND EXCHANGED FOR 'FREE' GOODS. SINCE THE 1990S, STORES HAVE ISSUED LOYALTY CARDS ON WHICH 'POINTS' ARE AMASSED, THEN USED FOR PURCHASE. THE BIGGEST ADVANTAGE TO THE STORE IS NOT THE MONETARY RECEIPTS BUT THE INFORMATION ON BUYING HABITS THAT CAN BE READ FROM THE CARD.

A GOOD GOSSIP

Now meaning the passer-on of tittle-tattle – either malicious or benign – the original gossip was a godparent or, in Old English, *godsibb*. That you should beware of gossip is summed up in the old Spanish proverb, 'Whoever gossips to you will gossip about you,' and in the saying that you should 'Count not him among your friends who will retail your privacies to the world.'

Referring back to the word's origin, 'sibbs' were not just brothers and sisters but also a woman's female friends, who remained with her during and after the birth of a child, and who – in the absence of other entertainment – would sit, chat and exchange news. The closest of this set would then be chosen as godparents.

THERE ARE SOME OTHER INTERESTING AND UNUSUAL WORDS ASSOCIATED WITH GOSSIP. IN YIDDISH TO GOSSIP IS TO *SCHMOOZE*, ESPECIALLY WHEN 'WORKING THE ROOM' AT A PARTY. A QUIDNUNC – FROM THE LATIN *QUID NUNC?* MEANING 'WHAT NOW?' – IS AN EXCEPTIONALLY INQUISITIVE PERSON.

According to the advice given to parents in the practical Victorian guidebook *Enquire Within*, there was a fine line to be drawn between gossip and a useful sense of curiosity. 'If you wish to cultivate a gossiping, meddling, censorious spirit in your children,' it advises, 'be sure when they come home from church, a visit, or any other place where you do not accompany them, to ply them with questions concerning what everybody wore, how everybody looked and what everybody said and did; and if you find anything in this to censure, always do it in their hearing.'

And, it continues, 'You will by this course render a spirit of curiosity, which is so early visible in children and which, if rightly directed, may be made the instrument of enriching and enlarging their minds, a vehicle of mischief which will serve only to narrow them.'

Among the many old opportunities for female gossip was the sewing bee. In the USA, especially, elaborate patchwork items, often depicting local folklore, were created at these intensely social gatherings.

PROMISES, PROMISES ...

Easy to make, promises are, it's said, 'like pie crusts, made to be broken'. In fact promises can be so hard to keep that for safety's sake it may be best to follow the advice of Napoleon Bonaparte who declared: 'The best way to keep one's word is not to give it.'

The Promise of Odin was, to Norsemen, the most binding of all oaths. As it was made, hands were shaken while being passed through either a silver ring or a sacrificial stone.

In dreams of future happiness, success – or even heaven – we may aim or yearn for the 'promised land'. In the Bible this was Canaan, the land promised by God to Abraham, Isaac and Jacob, which would be possessed by their offspring. It was to reach this desirable place that the Israelites, helped by the parting of the Red Sea, escaped from enslavement in Egypt to trek across the wilderness.

One of the greatest writers of proverbs, including the cautionary 'Never promise more than you can perform', was the Syrian slave Publilius Syrus

PROMISE PROVERBS

That there are so many sayings concerning promises is a tribute to their abundance, fragility and implications:

- Eggs and oaths are easily broken.
- A man apt to promise is apt to forget.
- Words and feathers the wind carries away.
- Men may promise more in a day than they will fulfil in a year.
- He loses his thanks that promises and delays.
- Promises may make friends but 'tis performances keeps them.
- An ox is taken by the horns, and a man by his word.

who, in the 1st century BC, was an author of mimes. These he acted out himself and they were so successful that, with his indubitable wit, they made him a favourite of Julius Caesar. As a reward the Emperor both freed and educated him.

'A LICK AND A PROMISE' IS AN EXPRESSION
FOR A PERFUNCTORY WASH.

KEEPING SECRETS

There are lots of good reasons for keeping secrets, not least because, according to the old proverb, 'He that tells a secret is another's servant.' The trouble that comes from breaking a secret's bond could even land you in gaol.

Skull and Bones, founded at Yale in 1832 by General William Huntington Russell and Alphonso Taft for the élite offspring of the Anglo-American Wall Street banking establishment, is one of the USA's most famous 'super-secret' societies. Its members include both President George W. Bush and his father.

Grandmother's advice that a secret shared is a secret betrayed still holds good today, the more so since e-mail has made it so easy to 'spread the word'. Stories abound of clandestine affairs being broadcast worldwide simply by mis-clicking the mouse. In an office situation this might be a sacking offence, but sign Britain's Official Secrets Act and then tell a secret – even if it is already in the public domain – and prosecution and a prison sentence are likely to ensue.

Secrets can legitimately be shared, however, in secret societies whose rules, rites and rituals are shared between members and disclosed to outsiders at members' peril. Initiation into such societies usually involves swearing an oath of allegiance (a practice roundly condemned by the Church when it involves the use of the Bible) and a clear indication of the social and material penalties that reneging on such an oath might involve.

The Eleusinian Mysteries were the most famous
secret religious rites of ancient Greece and related
to the story of Demeter, the earth goddess, who
went to Eleusis in search of her daughter Persephone, or Kore, after she was abducted by Hades,
god of the underworld. Neophytes were initiated
at the annual 'Lesser Mysteries' and six months
later the 'Greater Mysteries' celebrated Persephone's
return to earth. The initiates were forbidden ever to
speak of what took place. The promise of rewards
in the afterlife was a key benefit of belonging.

TACTFUL TALK

**Between silence and the full flow
of conversation comes the middle
ground where tact – the judicious
avoidance of insults – is crucial.
That people can be harmed by
words is a reminder of the linked
origins of 'tact' and 'touching'.**

*The word 'insult' comes
from the Latin meaning
'to jump on' and
originally referred to the
way you would jump on
to the already prostrate
form of an enemy.*

America's etiquette guru Emily Post had firm
opinions on the 'tactless blunder', declaring, 'If
you desire to be sought after, you must not talk
about the unattractiveness of old age to the elderly,
about the joys of dancing and skating to the lame,
or about the advantages of ancestry to the self
made.' And she adds, 'It is needlessly unkind to
ridicule or criticize others, especially for what
they can't help.'

Euphemisms or polite 'code' can be helpful in
situations where tact is essential. In the 1950s the
phrase 'Queen Anne's dead', said by one girl to

another, meant a petticoat showing beneath the
hemline. If a man was told 'You have egg on your
face' it was a signal to check that the fly in his
trousers was properly fastened.

The Irish writer and poet, W. E. Norris,
expressed the sentiment in verse:

If your lips would keep from slips,
Five things observe with care;
To whom you speak, of whom you speak,
And how, and when, and where.

THE ART OF CONVERSATION

**Once conversation begins, making the wrong
choice of what to say – and how to say it – can
land even the most mature of us in
trouble. Modern society's unwritten
rules are laxer than in the past,
when there were reams of rules to
learn, especially for children.**

*That we should temper
our conversation to our
audience is summed
up in the Malaysian
proverb: 'Trumpet in a
herd of elephants; crow
in the company of cocks;
bleat in a flock of goats.'*

Topics universally deemed uncom-
fortable for polite conversation are,
it is well known, politics and religion.
Beyond that, the Victorian manual
Enquire Within stressed that it was

important to make conversation interesting, advising that it should be enlivened by 'recitals calculated to impress your hearers', and to 'intersperse it with anecdotes and smart things'.

Emily Post warned the reader against being an 'unpleasant type' and identified such offenders in different categories, including the bore, 'one who insists on telling you at length something you don't want to hear about at all'; the wailer ('only your nearest and dearest care how many times you have been in the operating room'); the cutting wit, because 'sharp wit tends to produce a feeling of mistrust even while it stimulates'; the know-it-all; and the person who talks too much, because it is 'better to keep your mouth closed and be thought a fool than to open it and remove all doubts'.

AGAINST THE FOE

To have no enemies is a proverbial sign that 'fortune has forgot you': in reality none of us is devoid of enemies, even if they are largely confined to our own personal foibles or 'demons'.

Enemies can come in many guises. Wine, for instance, is '… a turncoat, first a friend, then an enemy'. They may be close at hand, and 'nothing is worse than a familiar enemy'. But an enemy may be useful if, as in the old Persian proverb, you can 'use his hand to catch a snake'.

The traditional way to deal with one's enemies was to wage war, and ancient societies invariably possessed war gods whose actions helped justify the attrition of their enemies. Most famous is Mars, to whom the Roman legionaries paid homage. His month, March, heralded the start both of spring and of annual campaigns against the enemies of Rome. On the battlefield soldiers would shout his name to strengthen their resolve.

By contrast, the role of the Chinese war god Guan Di was to prevent, not provoke, wars. Executed as a prisoner of war, he was officially recognized as a god relatively recently, in the year

> Contempt for an enemy was well expressed by the Greek philosopher Sophocles: 'Enemies' gifts are no gifts and do no good.'

1549. In a time of violence, he was revered for his courtesy and faithfulness as much as for his valour, and in Chinese temples he is still consulted about the outcome of future events.

In the poetic words of the 1662 Prayer Book, the Second collect for Peace runs:

O God, who art the author of peace and lover of concord, in knowledge of whom standeth our eternal life, whose service is perfect freedom; Defend us thy humble servants in all assaults of our enemies …

THE BEST HOSPITALITY

To welcome guests into your home is to share something valuable and important with them. For all to be well it is equally vital for guests never to outstay their welcome for, in the words of the 13th-century Florentine Guido Cavalcanti: 'A guest, like fish, has an unpleasant odour in three days.'

> 'If you are host to your guest' runs an old Russian proverb, 'be a host to his dog also.'

The pitfalls of entertaining are many. You must avoid at all costs, wrote Constance Cary Harrison in a 19th-century American guide, being 'The cold hostess; the distracted hostess …; the indifferent hostess, who, having spread her feast and set her people down to it, abandons them to their fate; the fussy hostess, interfering with talks happily begun; the affected hostess, apologizing for her banquet …'

Even in 1958, *Teach Yourself Etiquette and Good Manners* assumed that servants would help out the

> THE PINEAPPLE IS THE SYMBOL OF HOSPITALITY, AND IS
> OFTEN SEEN CARVED IN STONE AS AN ARCHITECTURAL
> MOTIF. ACCORDING TO AN AMERICAN LEGEND, THE
> SEA CAPTAINS OF THE CARIBBEAN RETURNED TO NEW
> ENGLAND BEARING PINEAPPLES, AND WOULD SPEAR THE
> FRUIT ON TO STAKES OUTSIDE THEIR HOMES TO LET THEIR
> FRIENDS KNOW THEY HAD ARRIVED HOME SAFELY AND AS
> AN INVITATION TO VISIT — AND CELEBRATE.

hostess at a formal dinner, and gave strict guidelines on the arrival and departure of guests (one servant taking ladies' coats, another the men's) and on the serving of food, beginning with the lady seated on the right of the host.

Advising guests staying overnight, or longer, the same guide stresses, in particular, that they 'should be punctual, avoid causing unnecessary work in the house, say in good time whether they intend to be in or out for a meal, and leave their hostess in no doubt either of the date and time of their arrival or of when they intend to leave.'

TROUBLE, TROUBLE

'A trouble shared is a trouble halved' runs the age-old advice – a sentiment endorsed by today's psychologists. And how to avoid trouble in the first instance? Don't go looking for it, or 'Never trouble trouble till trouble troubles you'.

Coping with trouble, especially some kind of loss or deprivation in early life, is an attribute shared by many successful entrepreneurs.

Sharing problems is what real friends are for, as well as being the basis of all the 'talking therapies'

> *The old-fashioned sewing bee, or today's knitting group, is the traditional women's forum for sharing troubles. As one American hobbyist aptly remarked: 'You can share an awful lot about yourself while unraveling 500 yards of worsted.'*

that aim to help people come to terms with and understand their problems. 'There is no problem,' says psychologist Dr Nick Baylis, 'that is not improved by asking for help.' And he goes on to assert that 'it is never too early [to ask for help]. As soon as trouble comes over the horizon that's the best time to call in the cavalry.'

When you are called upon to help a friend or relative in trouble, listening is the first requirement and, in the words of Ernest Hemingway, '... listen completely. Most people never listen.' Once that's done, then it may be time for action. Edgar Watson Howe, an American editor, novelist and essayist, had at least half the answer: 'When a friend is in trouble,' he advised, 'don't annoy him by asking if there is anything you can do. Think up something appropriate and do it.'

Trouble brewing? Before pronouncing their foul divinations to the ill-fated Macbeth, Shakespeare's witches stirred up their pot to this rhyme:

Double, double toil and trouble;
Fire burn and cauldron bubble ...
For a charm of powerful trouble,
Like a hell-broth boil and bubble.

THE PERFECT FRIENDSHIP

There is nothing quite like a best friend, the person you can tell everything to. Not only is friendship good for your health, but the friend in need truly is the 'friend indeed'.

A recent study conducted at the Harvard School of Public Health discovered that men with strong social ties had an 82 per cent lower chance of dying from heart disease than those who were more socially isolated, and the study's leading author,

Dr Eric Rimm, believes that the same is true for women. Anecdotal and scientific evidence bears these conclusions out.

There are psychological pluses too, in the personal growth and positive reassurance that friendship allows, even though friendship may sometimes demand hard work. Friendship can help keep depression at bay, while a word from a friend may be the push we need to solve a problem or make the changes in our lives that we've been putting off.

Money Matters

Ever since the scribes of ancient Mesopotamia compared the values of barley, wool and other commodities with a standard weight of silver, money has – more or less – made the world go round. Yet while money is useful, and its management a skill, having lots of it is by no means the password to contentment.

LOOK AFTER THE PENNIES

And the pounds (or dollars) will look after themselves, goes the old saying. The moral, of course, is that small savings will eventually add up to big ones, though those who take this to extremes are commonly regarded as miserly.

The word 'penny' comes from an early Germanic word meaning 'pledge', and Britain's first penny was introduced by

Egbert of Kent in the 8th century. The American one cent piece or penny (never its official name) was first minted from copper in 1793 in three designs: the Flowing Hair Chain, the Flowing Hair Wreath and the Liberty Cap. Since 1909 its obverse has carried the image of Abraham Lincoln.

Some of the wealthiest people in history have been famously careful about small expenditures. The multi-millionaire J. Paul Getty, who died in 1976, not only put payphones in the guest bedrooms of his mansion but insisted that his children use them also. Equally, there are many people who now make good livings from scouring skips and rubbish dumps for discarded, re-saleable valuables, from vintage clothes to scrap metal.

Penny banks – the first was founded in Scotland in 1847 – were a spur to the poor and the young to keep hold of what little extra money they had. Sunday Schools were particularly assiduous in encouraging junior savers.

NEITHER A BORROWER ...

... nor a lender be. 'For loan oft loses both itself and friend,' advises Polonius in Shakespeare's *Hamlet*. Borrowing money beyond one's means, and incurring the associated interest on loans unpaid, is also one of the great personal ills of modern life. At worst you may be declared bankrupt.

The word 'borrow' originally meant a pledge. In times past it was impossible to borrow money without leaving, on deposit, some valuable item that could be reclaimed only when the loan was repaid. That debts can be a many-faceted burden is borne out by experience and by numerous sayings, from 'Out of debt, out of danger' to 'Shame fades in the morning, but debts remain from day to day' and 'He that goes on borrowing goes on sorrowing.'

The Girls' Own Paper of July 1896, by way of a riddle, tells an amusing tale of borrowing entitled 'What the Halfpenny Did'. An office boy in London owed one of the clerks three-halfpence. The clerk owed the cashier a penny. The cashier owed the boy a penny. One day the boy paid the clerk one halfpenny on account. The clerk paid one halfpenny to the cashier. The cashier then paid the boy a halfpenny. The boy 'having his halfpenny again in hand' paid another third of his debt to the clerk. The clerk squared with the cashier, who instantly paid the boy in full. The lad then paid off the last of his debt of three-halfpence. 'Thus,' the tale concludes, 'were the parties square all round, and all their accounts adjusted.'

THE ART OF SHOPPING

Since shopping began thousands of years ago, quality and price have been deciding factors for the discerning shopper. In the 21st century, eBay has turned shopping, for some, from a necessity to an all-consuming activity.

Shopping originated when, in ancient Egyptian markets, people exchanged food and live animals for clothes, furniture and other necessities of life. As became the habit in medieval Europe, specialist traders would lay their goods out on the ground or on makeshift stalls. By the 12th century in Europe more permanent shops had been established, each specializing in a particular type of goods.

Having too much choice in the shops is one modern cause of stress – a condition the American psychologist Barry Schwartz has dubbed 'choice fatigue'. The happiest when presented with a multitude of choices, he maintains, are those he calls 'satisficers', who settle for something that is good enough, compared with the 'maximizers', who are driven always to seek out the best and will not settle for anything less than perfection.

The concept of the department store, selling 'Anything from a pin to an elephant' (which was the slogan of Whiteley's when it opened in London in 1863), began in Paris with the Belle Jardinière, opened in 1824. One famous pioneer of this type of shopping was the American Gordon Selfridge, whose innovations included annual sales and the placing of cosmetics counters near the front entrance of his store.

eBay, begun in 1995 when the French-Iranian computer programmer Pierre Omidyar built a website and auctioned off a broken laser pen for $14, has given rise to a business in which individuals are now turning over seven-figure sums every year from home. The most expensive item yet sold (in 2001) was a $4.9m Gulfstream II jet plane.

LUCK AND MONEY

Money has long been associated with good fortune, except for some particular denominations. The British five shilling piece or crown is thought to be unlucky, so is the American two dollar bill unless it is kissed or has a small piece torn off one corner.

To make money in business it is said that you should spit on the first ever coin you receive in a transaction and, if you are the owner of a store or restaurant, frame and display the first paper money you receive. On the personal side it's advisable, if you're superstitious, to put the first money you receive each day into an empty pocket.

Despite the popular saying 'See a penny pick it up, and all day you'll have good luck', the weight of opinion is that finding and keeping money is unlucky. Bad fortune may be dissipated if a coin lands 'heads up' or if you spit on it. And be careful when you give a gift of a purse. It will bring

COINS OF FORTUNE

What you do with money may have a lasting effect:

IT IS LUCKY TO:
- Toss a coin into a fountain (and you can make a wish).
- Carry a bent coin in your pocket.
- Wear a coin in your shoe if you are a bride.
- Carry a coin bearing your birth date.
- Keep a small coin in your purse.
- Put a small (money) spider in your pocket.
- Have a jar of pennies in the kitchen.

poverty, or all-round bad luck, unless you place a coin in it first.

Whether or not you have the makings of an entrepreneur may be down to the luck of your genetic inheritance. From studies of both identical twins and non-identical ones from deprived backgrounds, scientists assessing children's abilities have discovered that genetic factors are highly significant in determining their futures, including their ability to ascend from 'rags to riches'.

THE VALUE OF EVERYTHING

Though the earliest money consisted of coins made from precious metals, we now rely from day to day on monetary notes with their value printed on them in pounds, dollars or euros. However, 'The cynic,' said Oscar Wilde, 'is the man who knows the price of everything but the value of nothing.'

Metal coins were originally valued precisely by the amount of metal they contained. The reason why coins often have grooved or milled edges goes back to the common practice of shaving pieces of silver or gold from them, then melting it down and selling it. Although the Chinese invented paper money, probably around the 7th century, notes were not in common use in Europe until the 17th century. The Bank of England, which was

---

BE CAREFUL BEFORE YOU THROW AWAY THE 'JUNK' FROM YOUR ATTIC. IT MAY BE MORE VALUABLE THAN YOU THINK. A COPY OF *LIFE* MAGAZINE RECORDING THE FUNERAL OF JOHN F. KENNEDY CAN NOW COMMAND UP TO £80, A FIRST EDITION OF IAN FLEMING'S JAMES BOND NOVEL *FROM RUSSIA WITH LOVE* OVER £450. AN ENGLISH GOLDEN MOHAIR TEDDY BEAR FROM THE 1920s, WITH A JOINTED BODY, COULD BE WORTH WELL OVER £1,000.

---

founded to raise money for a war against the French, issued its first, numbered, handwritten notes in 1694. They could be redeemed for their cash value in whole or in part. Even today notes bear the legend 'I promise to pay the bearer on demand the sum of ...'

The first paper dollar bills date from 1785.

WHAT PRICE WEALTH?

There are many things in life that money cannot buy, not least our health and strength, and there are few who have not heard the Biblical warning that 'the love of money is the root of all evil'. But money can be useful, not only to make our lives more comfortable but to give to others.

The mythological Greek King Midas, as a favour for a good deed, was granted by Dionysus the ability to turn all that he touched to gold. But his joy quickly turned to horror when he discovered that even his food turned to the precious metal as he lifted it to his lips. According to legend, Dionysus agreed to purify him by allowing Midas to immerse himself in a river which forever thereafter was believed to contain gold dust.

'Be charitable,' was the advice of the Renaissance philosopher Sir Thomas Browne, 'before wealth makes thee covetous.' This is an eloquent reminder that we should share our riches with those less fortunate than ourselves. That many are prepared to do just that is borne out by the millions given in aid for the victims of the tsunami on 26 December 2004.

THE FRUGAL COOK

'A fat kitchen makes a lean will' goes the old saying, and cooks past and present will testify to the satisfaction of making the most of all their ingredients, throwing as little food as possible away and finding imaginative uses for anything left over.

Soups and stocks are the perfect way to make use of meat and poultry bones, and for odds and ends varying from a few carrots and mushrooms to the last handful of lentils in the jar. For centuries, homemade 'soup of the day' consisted of whatever happened to be in the kitchen stockpot, and even before science confirmed the antibacterial effects of heat, the sensible cook would make sure the

Growing your own is a great way to save money and to have fresh fruit and vegetables all the year round. As Mrs Beeton emphasized: 'To be acquainted with the periods when things are in season, is one of the most essential pieces of knowledge which enter into the "Art of Cookery".'

stock was thoroughly boiled each day to make it wholesome by killing food-poisoning germs.

Many famous cooks included recipes for 'warmed over' or *réchauffé* dishes in their repertoires. The 19th-century American guru Fannie Merritt Farmer recommended Cecils with Tomato Sauce – a type of croquette. Constance Spry, the English domestic goddess of the 1950s, favoured similar flat cakes 'containing a main cooked ingredient, bound together perhaps with potato or rice and moistened with milk, sauce or egg, then fried in shallow fat'.

PLANNING THE MENU

Working out the 'bill of fare' with cost in mind, especially for a large household, was a time-consuming task for the Victorian housewife. Enquire Within *recommends the following for 'a family of half a dozen':*

SUNDAY .... Roast beef and pudding.

MONDAY .... Fowl [chicken], what was left of pudding fried, or warmed in a Dutch oven.

TUESDAY .... Calf's head [extremely inexpensive], apple pie.

WEDNESDAY .... Leg of mutton.

THURSDAY .... Ditto broiled or hashed, and pancakes.

FRIDAY .... Fish pudding.

SATURDAY .... Fish, or eggs and bacon.

Against Time

'Gain time, gain life' goes the old saying. So why is it that when we're having fun time flies by too fast, but when we're bored or depressed it ticks by at a snail's pace? Though it can now be measured down to the nanosecond, this remains the mystery of the fourth dimension.

THE OLD ENEMY

Ask 'How goes the enemy?' and you'd expect someone in the know to tell you the time. The passing minutes are our adversary when they tick away faster than we would like for, as is well known, 'Time and tide wait for no man'.

Our concept of time in its most basic form of day and night comes from the movement of the earth around the sun. From observing the movements of the sun across the sky, the ancient Egyptians were the first to segment the year into 12 months and to divide each day into two 12-hour periods. During daylight hours time's passage was recorded on sundials; after dark by measuring the movements of the stars and with water clocks.

The superstitious often take particular note of time. A clock that strikes the wrong time is thought to be an evil omen, as is meeting a clergyman in the morning.

By the Middle Ages, timekeeping had become important to monks, who were called to prayer by church bells, but it was centuries later, with the advent of railway timetables in the 1830s (notably George Bradshaw's 1839 charting of all Britain's railway services) that it became essential for clocks to tell the same time in different places.

THE PRESSURES OF MODERN LIFE MAKE US SLAVES TO OUR DEADLINES, BUT THE WORD HAS A MORE MACABRE MEANING. THE TREACHEROUS CURRENT TWO MILES ABOVE NIAGARA FALLS IS KNOWN AS THE DEADLINE. ONCE A BOAT HAS MOVED INTO THIS AREA, OR A SWIMMER HAS ALLOWED THEMSELVES TO BE SWEPT THERE, BOTH ARE DOOMED.

THE GREAT HEALER

Time, that is. It is said to 'tame the strongest grief' or even 'cure all things'. For physical ills, overnight cures are indeed the exception, not the rule, while for mental torment in general, and bereavement in particular, time has proved to be our most valuable asset.

The human body is equipped with a remarkable armoury of self-repair systems, which work at different speeds. If you cut yourself, for instance, it normally takes only about ten minutes for blood to clot, beginning the process of sealing the wound. Quickly, white blood cells begin engulfing germs and dirt, cleaning things up, but even for a small cut it will take a week, at least, for skin to heal over.

'THE LONGER IT IS KEPT THE BETTER IT WILL BE' IS, AS GOOD COOKS KNOW, THE MAXIM FOR MATURING PICKLES AND CHUTNEYS. BECAUSE OF THE GERM-KILLING POWERS OF THEIR CONSTITUENT VINEGAR AND SALT, HOMEMADE PRESERVES CAN STILL BE FIT TO EAT AFTER 30 YEARS AND MORE.

The custom for formal mourning reached its height in the 19th century. Typically widows were expected to undertake, in their dress at least, 'two years of deep mourning, in which the only wear is woollen stuffs and crape'.

Loss of a loved one – through death, divorce or any other reason – demands, for healing, a period of mourning, in which emotions can range through (usually in this order) numbness and anger to tearfulness, anxiety and depression. But a 2005 report from America's Center for the Advancement of Health surprisingly concluded that most grieving people do not need or benefit from bereavement counselling or any kind of intervention, and that these can even disrupt the grieving process.

RHYTHMS OF LIFE

Why does time drag when we're young and race when we're old? Why are some of us sprightly, sunrise people, others at their best at two in the morning? Much, say the scientists, has to do with the way we respond to natural rhythms.

That children have a different perception of time's passing than adults may have as much to do with their body metabolism as their mental maturity. Because, it's argued, children have higher metabolic rates and process information more quickly, they are likely to perceive that a week is as long as a year (especially when it's nearly Christmas or a birthday). For older people, with slower metabolisms, the reverse is true.

While today we struggle with time management and multi-tasking, for our forebears – especially women in rich households – time was often overabundant. The members of a Victorian family would amuse themselves by the fireside with 'Anagrams, Arithmorems, Single and Double Acrostics ... Charades, Conundrums ... Rebuses [and] Riddles' and more.

TIME FLIES WHEN YOU'RE HAVING FUN BECAUSE YOUR MIND IS SO ENGAGED THAT YOU'RE UNAWARE OF THE PASSING MINUTES.

Whether you're a lark or an owl – or somewhere between the two – depends on your personal body clock, though even for owls, mental performance (measured by ability at mental arithmetic) is better in the morning. Overriding our natural preference, however, is our response to the daily rhythm of light and dark. That it is important to respond to this cosmic discipline is born out by studies suggesting that children exposed to light during the night may be at a greater risk from cancer because the functioning of their immune systems is disrupted.

THE TIME OF YEAR

The poet T. S. Eliot declared that April was the cruellest month – but residents of temperate climes are more likely to get the blues in winter, not least because lack of sunshine can be a real cause of depression.

Between October and April each year, about 2 per cent of the UK population suffer from severe symptoms of SAD, or seasonal affective disorder, brought about by lack of sunshine, and this figure is closely mirrored in other countries where winter light levels are low. Physiologically, the reason is that the hypothalamus at the base of the brain is insufficiently stimulated, affecting the proper control of hormone production, which in turn affects sleep, appetite and mood.

Spring, when, as Tennyson put it, '… a young man's fancy/Lightly turns to thoughts of love', is nature's favoured time for birth, giving young animals warmth and the maximum chance of abundant food. While human babies born in spring are generally the healthiest, one recent study suggests that for brainpower, being born in autumn is best.

Dr Cliff Arnall of Cardiff University has calculated that in Britain 24 January is the most depressing day of the year, when debts, broken New Year resolutions and bad weather combine to make us feel lowest.

USE IT OR LOSE IT

Exercising the brain is the surest way to keep the ravages of time at bay and enjoy a fit old age. Practice still makes perfect, however many years you have on the clock. As life spans increase we all hope to postpone as long as possible the state of being 'sans everything'.

Medical experts agree: keep your intellect well honed, pursue creative and mind-stretching activities and you have the best chance of avoiding Alzheimer's disease. As one John Adams once said 'Old minds are like old horses; you must exercise

Keep your memory well honed, but don't be a bore, like the old person described by Emily Post as 'a clinging questioner' who 'won't let any approach of friendliness end without asking for a complete report on the health and occupation of every relative …'

them if you wish to keep them in working order.' To keep the body in tip-top condition, exercise is key to help keep joints supple and muscles toned. Weight-bearing exercise has the bonus of keeping bone density levels high and helping to ward off osteoporosis.

CHOOSE YOUR MOMENT

Timing can be everything. However, the proverb writers are contradictory in their advice, for while 'There is a time and place for everything' it is also said that in some circumstances it is unwise to act too quickly, as in 'Marry in haste, repent at leisure'.

For gardeners, ever at the mercy of the weather, choosing the moment can be critical to success or failure. Put your tender annuals out too early and they'll be ruined by spring frost. Wait too long to plant your seeds and your late crops will be cut short by autumn cold.

Life is forever a toss-up between acting promptly to avert trouble – and waiting to see how things pan out. Experience helps, but sometimes we just have to follow our instincts and take the consequences. However, it is always wise (though not always possible) to think before you speak, and it's good manners not to interrupt the conversations of others.

The importance of good timing, and the consequences of poor choice, are illustrated in Aesop's *Fables* in the tale of 'The Young Wastrel and the Swallow': 'Having squandered his inheritance, a young wastrel possessed only his cloak. He noticed a swallow who had arrived early, so, thinking that summer had come, he took off his cloak and sold that too. But wintry weather was still to come. It grew very cold. He was out walking one day when he came across the swallow, frozen to death. He said: "Miserable wretch! You've ruined us both at once."'

THE IDEA THAT YOU SHOULD SEIZE THE DAY (*CARPE DIEM*) ORIGINATED WITH THE ROMAN POET HORACE. 'REJOICE WHILE YOU ARE ALIVE,' HE SAID, 'ENJOY THE DAY; LIVE LIFE TO THE FULLEST; MAKE THE MOST OF WHAT YOU HAVE. IT IS LATER THAN YOU THINK.'

Perchance to Dream

The need for sleep – and dreams – is intrinsic to the human condition. Without it our memories, mental equilibrium and even our personalities are disturbed. So vivid are our nightly 'visions' that their interpretation and symbolism have for centuries been the subject of intense analysis and speculation.

TIRED AND WEARY

Despite our plethora of modern conveniences, fatigue is a common affliction for young and old alike. If insomnia is your problem, there are lots of helpful treatments that have been tried and tested over the years.

To stop them tiring on their journeys, medieval travellers would carry with them mugwort ointment, made by mixing the herb with lard, to put on their feet or in their shoes, or would drink the juice of the plant from empty eggshells. In doing so, they were following a tradition recorded by Pliny in the first century AD and protecting themselves against the other evils mugwort was believed to keep at bay, including thunder, lightning and blindness.

AN EASY WAY TO GET OVERTIRED IS TO BURN THE CANDLE AT BOTH ENDS. THE EXPRESSION WAS USED BY THE POETESS EDNA ST VINCENT MILLAY IN THE VERSE: 'MY CANDLE BURNS AT BOTH ENDS;/IT WILL NOT LAST THE NIGHT;/BUT, AH, MY FOES, AND OH, MY FRIENDS –/IT GIVES A LOVELY LIGHT.'

Health advisers of the 1930s warned against a condition dubbed 'brain fag', brought on by overworking the brain. 'If the condition is well developed,' said the *Concise Household Encyclopedia*, 'the patient must rest.' To prevent the symptoms that we recognize today, including 'impaired memory, loss of pleasure in work and recreation', it recommended the accepted 21st-century remedy of exercise, physical fitness, a good diet and plenty of sleep.

A GOOD EIGHT HOURS

'Sleep,' said an anonymous Chinese sage, 'is a priceless treasure; the more one has of it the better it is.' Essential to refresh the body and brain, sleep keeps the memory in trim and even helps prevent illness and accidents.

Although many people manage on less, average adults – whatever their age – need around seven hours of sleep a night, with at least two periods each of deep and REM (rapid eye movement) sleep, during which dreaming happens. Deprived of sleep, our immune systems become weakened, production of the stress hormone cortisol is increased (impairing the memory), and our abilities with logic and problem solving decrease. Increased is the likelihood of having a car accident, because as well inducing drowsiness, sleep deprivation is detrimental to both our reflexes and response times. Tell-tale signs that you're not getting enough sleep include

Yawning is the body's reflex response to tiredness – and boredom. A yawn ups the amount of oxygen getting into the lungs and increases blood circulation to the brain, but no one has yet explained why yawning is so contagious.

needing the alarm clock to wake up in the morning, nodding off during the day, irritability, blurred vision, confusion and poor recall. If night-time hours aren't enough, the power nap can help. One 2002 Harvard study found that naps, ideally of 20 to 30 minutes a day, timed at least four hours before bed, increased productivity by as much as 30 per cent.

ACCORDING TO THE AMERICAN FABLE CREATED BY WASHINGTON IRVING, RIP VAN WINKLE FELL ASLEEP AFTER DRINKING FROM A KEG WHICH HE HELPED A DWARF CARRY UP A MOUNTAIN IN THE CATSKILLS. WHEN HE WOKE 20 YEARS LATER THE WORLD WAS TRANSFORMED. HIS GUN WAS RUSTED, HIS DOG DEPARTED AND THE CIVIL WAR HAD BEEN AND GONE.

SWEET DREAMS

Dreams are a necessity – not just for refreshment but to allow us vital time for mental reassessment. During dreams our brains analyse, process and sift information about our lives past, present and future, and try to come to terms with our anxieties.

Enjoy your dreams but don't necessarily treat them as true, for to believe in your dreams is, it's said, to spend all your life asleep.

When we dream, whether in colour or black and white, our eyes move beneath their closed lids, our breathing becomes fast, irregular and shallow. And whether we're having a pleasurable dream or a raging nightmare, our hearts beat faster and our blood pressure rises. Though most dreams are forgotten, it is possible to train yourself to remember them.

DAYDREAMING IS, SAY THE EXPERTS, A USEFUL MENTAL TOOL WHEN APPROPRIATELY USED. CREATIVITY IS BELIEVED TO BE HEIGHTENED WHEN THE CONSCIOUS BRAIN IS IN A STATE OF 'SEMI-ENGAGEMENT'.

Aside from the rigours of psychoanalysis, interpreting your dreams can give useful clues to your anxieties and needs. To do this you need to keep a dream diary, recording the people and places they contain, and significant life events and concerns of the past 24 hours. By relating your dreams to your life concerns, you can create links between the two. It is also possible to identify underlying and deep-seated anxieties and desires – even those in your unconscious mind.

THE LANGUAGE OF DREAMS

The symbolism of dreams is a subject that has engaged people since ancient times. More recently it has become significant in the analysis of human problems, desires and personality. Countless interpretations exist, however, for the meanings of the images that appear in dreams.

Soldiers in World War I, marching to an uncertain future, sang the song written by Stoddart King 'There's a long, long trail a-winding/Into the land of my dreams.'

Dreams, believed Sigmund Freud, the 'father' of psychoanalysis, are hidden repressed wishes (often of a sexual nature) and residues of the day's activities which, in the dream, become interlinked with unconscious wishes. The objects that occur in a dream are, he said, unacceptable or threatening thoughts transformed into an 'appropriate manifestation'. He also believed

DREAM OBJECTS

An 18th-century pamphlet 'The Old Egyptian fortune-Teller's Last Legacy', included many dream objects and their meanings, including:

VERMIN AND TROUBLE KILLING THEM	Riches
FLYING	Praise
FALLING FAR WITHOUT BEING HURT	Fortune is at hand
A RING THAT FALLS OFF YOUR FINGER OR HAVING TEETH DRAWN	Loss of a friend
MUSIC	Impending marriage
NOSEBLEED	Impending doom
CROSSING A RIVER	Hard labour in store

that the most insights come from the most insignificant parts of the dream. Carl Jung, by contrast, looked directly at what dreams reveal, believing that dreams represent current situations in the dreamer's life. He saw them as guides to our waking life, and looked to the myths and legends of the past to find common themes that have occurred in dreams throughout human history.

DREAMING OF THE FUTURE

In ancient civilizations, dreams were thought of as one of the important means by which the gods communicated with humans, and a way that humans might learn what was in store for them. In more modern times, the evidence suggests that it may be wise to heed the warnings of dreams.

In 1847, in Kennebunkport, Maine, one Thomas King signed on as crew member of the ship Isidore *but, before it sailed, dreamed of a shipwreck, and of seven men dead on the deck. He refused to put to sea. Not only were the ship and 15 crew lost, but when the ship was found there were indeed seven bodies on the deck.*

For Egyptian kings, dreams were thought to underlie their power. In the 15th century BC, the future Pharaoh Thutmose I fell sleep during a hunting expedition in the shade of an image of Harmakhis (a representation of Ra, the sun god). In his dream, Harmakhis not only told the sleeping prince that he would give him a long and prosperous reign but advised him to take note of the sorry state of his image, the Sphinx, which lay half buried in the sand. Not only did Thutmose become king, but he also 'rescued' the Sphinx.

The ancient Greeks believed Zeus, king of the gods, to be the bringer of dreams. In a dream, visits to the sleeping person could be made by a dream figure or *oneiros*, who could be a god, a ghost or a specially created image or *eidolon* that took on the form of a person known to the sleeper. From this came oneiromancy, the study of dream divination, one of the earliest written records of which was by St Nicephorus, a 9th-century patriarch of Constantinople.

Index

Page numbers in **bold** refer to headings; numbers in *italic* refer to sections